ANDAMAN AND NICOBAR ISLANDS

ANDAMAN AND NICOBAR ISLANDS
A Saga of Freedom Struggle

R.V.R. Murthy

KALPAZ

Andaman and Nicobar Islands
A Saga of Freedom Struggle

ISBN: 978-81-7835-903-8

Published in 2011 in India by
Kalpaz Publications
C-30, Satyawati Nagar,
Delhi-110052
E-mail: kalpaz@hotmail.com
Phone : 9212729499

Lasser Type Setting : Quick Media, Delhi
Printed at : Chawla Offset Printers, Delhi

Dedicated
to the sacred memories of all the
freedom fighters of Andaman Islands

Contents

Preface

The saga of freedom struggle is perhaps the first great movement of mankind in the twentieth century. The achievement of Indian freedom from the British yoke, was a unique experience having its origin way back to the First War of Independence of 1857. Giving their prime youth for the sake of their motherland was an extraordinary contribution ever any nation had experienced in the world. The spirit of Indian Freedom Movement was immense, the ritual of the spinning-wheel (of non-violence) and the swooping-sword (of violence), pervaded and influenced all walks of Indian life. The influence came through direct participation of people regardless of their social obligations in the movement by manifesting their strength in consolidation of one nation. In the beginning, the influence crystallized in the form of passionate appreciation of everything Indian caused emergence of different thoughts within the purview of nationalism.

Capital punishment in British colonial India was not just a method of crime control or individual punishment, but an integral aspect of colonial hegemony of power and violence. The treatment of anti-state activist and the rituals of execution which brought their lives to an end illustrate the tensions within colonialism surrounding the relationship between the state and their subjects. The state may have had the legal right to kill its subjects, but this right and the manner in which it was enacted were contested. This book explores the interactions between various actors in the penal 'theatre of death', looking at the motivations behind changing phases of the death penalty, the treatment of the condemned political prisoners whilst they awaited death, and the performance of a hanging itself to show how British colonial governments in Andaman Islands attempted to create and manage the deaths of their condemned subjects. Under the "Bloody Code", the British courts adopted transportation as an alternative for a punishment which was not as extreme as hanging, but tougher than a fine. In the absence of proper prisons, transportation seemed the answer. For this Andaman islands were used for over a hundred years. Many political prisoners viewed that the transportation to Andaman Islands was much more humiliating, harder, hellish and a form of extreme highhandedness of the British colonialists on the intellectual class than capital punishment.

The Andaman Islands are very intimately associated with the Indian Freedom Movement ever since it began in 1857. Innumerable political prisoners were jailed in galos and every act of these great sons conveys the spirit of national unity and integrated struggle for the salvation of India. The freedom fighters, who were brought to the Andaman Islands, can be roughly divided into three phases. The first included the rebels of the 1857 struggle; the second the political prisoners between 1910 to 1921; and third, the political prisoners between 1932 to 1937. Records pertaining to the first phase are scanty or completely missing. However, it is known with certainty that Maulana Liaquat Aly (Ali), the leader of 1857 struggle died here. Other prominent person, were Allami Fazil Haq 'Khairabadi, Ramnauth, Shewdeen, Mohammud Bux , Koonj Baharee, Ahbar Ali, Khoda Bux, Koor Singh, Mohammed Jan, Hurdeo Singh, Juggur Nath, Panchum Singh and others. Heroes of 1857 struggle were brutally punished and inflicted with the great horror of being exiled. From Assam, Dante Ram Barman, Sheikh Formud Ali, Madhu Malik and Bahadurgoan Burah were also transported to Kala Paani. The punishment was intolerable and a perpetual victimization fully in human.

The second phase of prisoners started with the Alipore Conspiracy Case in 1908. Except for Aurobindo Ghosh who was acquitted, the other four suspects were sentenced to transportation for life to these islands. In 1911, another well known name, Vinayak Damodar Savarkar of the Nasik Conspiracy Case was sentenced to transportation for life. Noni Gopal Mukherjee was sentenced to 14 years of imprisonment and sent to the islands following the Dalhousie Square bomb case. The life for these prisoners was extremely hard since they had to help run the daily affairs of the islands. They were expected to help in construction activities, keeping the settlement and the jail clean, and do many more activities in addition to these. But for all this, they still received very inhuman treatment from the British. This fact is amply illustrated by the suicide committed by Indu Bhushan Roy in 1912 (a young freedom fighter from Bengal). In another case, Ulaskar Dutt who was convicted in the Alipore Conspiracy, turned insane. Consequent to these tragic happenings, Ladha Ram who had edited the *Swarajya*, a nationalist weekly, went on a hunger strike protesting against the prevailing inhuman conditions. In the following years, between 1913 and 1914, the jail saw further protests in the form of hunger strikes. Somewhere around this period the records tell us, Bhai Paramananda and Ashutosh Lahiri resorted to violent tactics and threw a European jailer down. By 1919-1920 things had deteriorated further and the Indian Jail Committee appointed a committee to look into the atrocities committed by the jail authorities, which finally Sir William Vincent, Home Secretary to the Government of India decided to abolish and sent all the prisoners back to India by 1921. Virtually the islands were abandoned and all the political prisoners sent to mainland jails. No more political convicts were sent for transportation to Andaman Islands. Meanwhile the British authorities were under constant pressure by the local born population not to vacate the islands because of the social stigma associated with them. To re-introduce the island society, a fresh offer of colonization scheme was launched and encouraged to bring homogeneous communities like Moplahs, Karen and Bhantus suitable to adverse climatic conditions and to improve agricultural production as well as to cater from the Indian sub-continent, its maritime interest in the middle of the Bay of Bengal.

Transportation resumed only in 1932 due to fresh violence and the number of prisoners hovered around 300. Kamalnath Tewari, Batukeshwar Dutt, Mahabir Singh, Kundan Lal and Dr. Gaya Prasad, all prisoners of Lahore Conspiracy Case were deported to the Andamans in January 1933. Jai Dev Kapoor, Bejoy Kumar Sinha and Sheo Verma reached the Andamans in June 1933. However, following the 1937 elections which were swept by the Indian National Congress, there was heavy unrest in the jails and mass protests by way of hunger strikes. The political prisoners started agitating against the barbaric and inhuman behaviour of the British authority. There were few hunger strikes by individuals and groups, and other minor incidents which kept alive the sentiments of nationalism among the inmates of the jail. Some heroic acts and slogans raised in the jail were crushed with high-handedness. Perhaps the British thought that the cry of the political prisoners will remain confined to the islands and even its ethos would be lost in the roaring waves of the sea extended to miles together. They were greatly astonished when despite the strict watch over the political prisoners, they were able to send tales of their woes and sufferings to the mainland. Indeed this news created tremendous uproar in the entire country. In their sympathy and support the other freedom fighters undergoing imprisonment in different jails of the country, also went on hunger strikes. Ultimately the Government was compelled to repatriate all political prisoners to the mainland and by January 1938 the Cellular Jail was denuded of all these freedom fighters.

The spirit of fighting against injustice, implied in the Independence Movement, has been pervading the minds of younger generations of Andaman Islands when the Second World War broke out. Japanese forces occupied the British controlled Andaman Islands in 1942. They met no resistance from the local population but within hours the 'Sons of Heaven' started an orgy of looting, raping and murder. Unbelievable orgies were perpetrated in the towns and villages with women and young girls forcibly raped and young boys sodomized. In Port Blair, eight high-ranking Indian officials were tortured then buried up to their chests in pits they were forced to dig. Their chests, heads and eyes were then prodded with bayonets after which the pit was sprayed with bullets until the helpless victims were all dead. The Director of Health and President of the Indian Independence League, Diwan Singh, was arrested and nearly 2000 of his Peace Committee associates incarcerated in the local jail and subjected to the water treatment, electric shocks and other unspeakable forms of torture for eighty-two days. Those left alive were then taken out to the country and shot and buried. After the massacre, the Japanese resorted to a reign of terror, women were abducted and taken to the officers club to be raped by the officer elite. A shipload of Korean girls was brought in to participate in this 'sport'. During the three and a half years of Japanese occupation, out of the 40,000 population of Port Blair around 30,000 were brutally murdered. The small islands of the Andamans were left a scene of utter devastation. This indeed was Japan's way of helping India get her freedom from British rule!

The real spirit and zeal of freedom was celebrated when Subhas Chandra Bose hoisted the tri colour at Port Blair on 30th December' 1943. The patriotic feelings of the Islanders have portrayed and glorified every aspect concerning the leaders and freedom struggle. The Andaman Islands' contribution was undermined in the annals of history of Indian national movement. Indeed this book highlights the sacrifices of unsung, unheard heroes of our freedom struggle, who laid down life for the sake of the freedom of their motherland. This is an attempt to justify that the Andaman Islands were closely connected with the saga of India's freedom struggle and exonerated great contribution towards national spirit which is primary source for inspiration for present generations.

This book seeks to reflect the desire of a teacher to emphasize the significance of the saga of freedom struggle in Andaman Islands. 'My interest in colonial politics of Andaman Islands is genuine and in the implication of that political struggle for nationalism was deepened by subsequent investigations on extremist nationalism, which was my area of research for Ph.D degree.' Further this book presents contribution of Andaman Islands within the framework of Indian nationalism which was instrumental in posing challenge to British colonial regime despite of adversity and authority, the spirit of political prisoners never ceased and they were ready to accept death for the sake of salvation of motherland. In writing this book have been fortunate in being able to get wide range of help. I take this opportunity to extend my sincere gratitude to all my well wishers and friends. I also gratefully acknowledge the assistance which I received on various occasions from the staff of National Archives, New Delhi, Lucknow Secretariat Records Room, R.B.S. College Library, Agra, Dr. B.R. Ambedkar University Library, Agra, Jawaharlal Nehru University Library, New Delhi, India Centre, New Delhi, Connemara Public Library, Chennai, Cellular Jail Library, State Library, and Secretariat Archives at Port Blair. I am grateful for their kindness and cooperation. My special acknowledgement to all the local born community especially those who had lent moral support to the project. They deserve a word of appreciation.

The manuscript was guided to publication by Gyan Publishers, New Delhi, who gave strong encouragement when I needed it most. My special thanks to Kalpaz Publication, Delhi, for readily agreeing to publish this volume and bringing it out most efficiently.

Finally, I owe a great deal to my wife, sons and mother, whose patience and encouragement were a source of inspiration to me. To be aided in one's scholarship is not to share responsibility for it. I alone am responsible for what is written in these pages and I would be anxious to know how far this book conveys to the readers the unique contribution of Andaman Islands in the annals of the freedom struggle in India.

R.V.R. Murthy

1
Introduction

Transportation has been used as a form of punishment since 1717 by the British colonialists to isolate the native political aspirants from the mainstream politics. Under the "Bloody Code"[1] (See Gallery Crime 1750-1900), courts were looking for a punishment which was not as extreme as hanging, but tougher than a fine. In the absence of proper prisons, transportation seemed the answer and was used for over a hundred years in the Indian sub-continent to crush the anti-nationalists. Many political prisoners were transported to the fare-ast settlements including Andaman Islands to execute a hard type of punishment under liberal laws. They were sent first to the "hulks"(disused warships). Conditions on these rotting vessels were often terrible, with death rates of one in three. Prior to Andaman penal settlement, the long voyage to Benkulu, Penang, Melaka and Singapore and the Burmese provinces of Arakan and Tenasserim (1828-62) could take a week together to reach such far flung penal colonies. Many lives were lost among the prisoners, locked in iron cages below decks in insanitary conditions. Removing political prisoners from the mainland did not seem to have had any effect on the nationalist aspirations, rather it created more youth brigades which were mobilized in the process of India's struggle for independence.[2] Prisons were considered a better method of punishing or reforming detainees, many new ones were being built across the Indian sub-continent to execute severity of anti-imperialist crimes. Nonetheless, the Andaman Islands were prominent among different jails across the country due to their geo-physical isolation from rest of the Indian sub-continent. Prominent jails in Andaman islands were Viper island Jail, Mount Harriet Jail, female jail and the infamous Cellular Jail. Infact, the British used these islands as a dumping-ground for criminals and anti-nationals. Later it turned to be a sociological experiment for accommodating communities within the realm of society.

Reading the memories of political detainees of Andaman Islands as per the available records across the country reveals that a large number of political prisoners were inflicted unimaginable punishments to create fear in their minds showing a horrible state of authoritarianism. Reading the history of transportation from the perspective of the Indian Penal system and law-making can perhaps provide a deeper understanding of the ideological role that each punishment played.[3] The prison history of Andaman Island was remarkable in terms of nationalism and colonial enterprise for two reasons. Firstly, the colonial interest was secured by expanding their territory to far away places including fleet extension to control sea lines to Fareast Asia. Secondly, the island region served as an ideal place to crush the sentiments of nationalism by isolating the intellectual class, who were predominant in leading the national movement by their indigenous writings and appealing for active participation. The worst face of colonialism was witnessed especially on political prisoners who were deported to the Andaman Islands in the post-mutiny of 1857 and subjected untold humiliation.

The British rulers embraced a continually tougher stance on political crimes - demanding longer sentences and tougher conditions, in the belief that such measures would deter the problem of political crimes especially in India in the post-mutiny of 1857. With this intention the British were selective to colonize certain territories in the Fareast to isolate the intellegencia as well as other anti-nationals from Indian society. The most infamous prison in the Indian history, was a desolate place of exile in the Bay of Bengal which was actually a small island, over time, became known collectively as 'Andaman Islands'. During its existence as a penal colony

(1858-1945), more than 36,000 prisoners were transported there. Of this number, perhaps one-fourth returned to mainland. The group of islands was collectively and popularly known by the name Andaman Islands and formed a penal colony notorious for its terrible conditions. Later, as a result of atrocities committed by British on the political detainees, the prison was referred to as the 'Kalapani' or 'island of death'. To crush patriotic sentiments of nationalists the Cellular Jail system, which was based on 'Aborn system' was introduced to isolate political detainees' from the rest of the community; adopted a firm policy of solitary confinement in tiny, dark cells and cages to bring down the scale of politically motivated crimes in the Indian sub-continent. The Cellular Jail was built in 1906, originally to introduce stringent corrective reforms to prisoners associated with dangerous criminal activities. Nonetheless, the entire island region was developed as a natural jail in which the political prisoners were injected most heinous methods of punishment which was shameful for the entire mankind for centuries together, where the political prisoners were subdued by solitary confinement in tiny, dark cells; some times they were put inside cages alike animals.

Thousands of the less imaginative political prisoners persisted by receiving excessive punishment in the form of hard work amidst climatic adversity. The penalty for failing to escape was horrific. Three attempts to escape resulted in a classification of "Incorrigible." After completing their formal punishment in solitary confinement, such "incos" were banished to the most dreaded camps where they worked like beasts all day; at night, they were placed in iron cells until the following morning. The determination to escape at all costs illustrates a human spirit that would rather suffer than endure life on the "islands of death," as the prisoners called them. The imponderable element in any man's ability to survive was the quality of character exhibited in the face of impossible adversity.

The introduction of the prison system in Andaman Islands has a distinct element of historical and colonial excessiveness on helpless colonial people. These islands were being used as distant or overseas settlement established to punish criminals including political activists through forced labour and isolation from society was historical blunder.

The Penal colony was also associated with the term 'transportation for life', which involved sending a convict into banishment or exile. This had been authorized as one form of punishment for certain serious crimes by the Europeans under the "General Regulations".[4] The kinds of punishments were purposely structured to be harsh in an attempt to deter future offenders. Indeed penal order was developed into a major part of the British correctional system in the nineteenth century. It was not until the first half of the nineteenth century that imprisonment became a conventional form of punishment in Europe and North America. Nevertheless imprisonment as a form of punishment was more common in England than on the European continent.[5] Enough records prove that such penal colonies were developed mostly by the English, French, and Russians to inject necessary social obligations to socially manageable and law-abiding class.

Britain sent criminals to its American colonies until the eighteenth century; Australia was principally a penal colony from its colonization until the mid-19th century.[6] French Guiana, site of a French penal colony, was infamous for its inhumanity; 'Devil's Island', existed up to World War II. Russian penal colonies were established in Siberia under the Tsars but were most widely used during the Stalin era. In colonial India, the British had made various penal colonies later turned to be penal settlements to fulfill their maritime interest as well as to safeguard economic interest. Two of the most infamous ones in the Indian sub-continent were on the 'Andaman Islands' and 'Hijli'.[7] Notorious for their harsh punishments and underfeeding, most penal colonies have now been abolished. The British used Andaman Islands as a penal colony both in the usual sense and through the system of indentured servitude. Convicts would be transported by private sector merchants and auctioned off to plantation owners upon arrival in the colonies. The British started the system of the transportation of Indian prisoners to an overseas penal settlement in 1787. Lord Cornwallis sent the first batch of Indian convicts into banishment to Benkoelen in Southwest Sumatra in 1787.[8]

Early History of Transportation in South–East Asia

In the initial years of the American War of Independence (1778), Britain was undergoing social upheaval. It manifested itself through massive agricultural, industrial and social change. With the gradual withdrawal of their hegemony in the northern American continent on their was faced with overcrowded prisons and prison ships and no suitable destination to transport their convicts to far off places. Lieutenant James Cook's discovery and annexation for Britain of the east coast of Australia in 1770, aroused new interest. Some of these early colonies were Norfolk Islands, Van Diemen's Land and New South Wales.[9]

In the beginning of the eighteenth century a penal colony was established at South-east Asia, where convicts were directly sent from India. Such colonies were established in the vicinity of the Indian sub-continent to fulfill their economic interest as well as hidden strategy to isolate the criminals and anti-nationalists from mainstream politics and they were viz., Panang (1796), Mauritius (1817), Moulmien and Tenassarim (1822) and Malacca (1826) few were well-known in the history. The Anglo-Dutch Treaty 1824 created two spheres of influence in the East Indies-British and Dutch. British Bencoolen was exchanged for Dutch Malacca so that Penang, Malacca and Singapore came under British influence in the Malay Peninsula.[10] When Bencoolen was vacated, the British transferred the Indian convicts to Singapore in 1826. The convicts first occupied the Temenggong's Village (vacated by the Temenggong who moved out to Telok

Blangah) near the Singapore River. Later they moved to permanent buildings erected for them between Bras Basah Road and Stamford Road. At one time there were about 2000 convicts. They were deployed as labourers for the Public Works Department and were generally well-behaved and hard-working; they were supervised by their own fellow convicts. The convicts contributed much towards the early development of Settlement and they build some of the most beautiful buildings existing today - the Istana and St Andrew's Cathedral; they build early roads and filled up swamps to create Commercial Square (Raffles Place), Thomson Road and Bukit Timah. There were stone cutters for the Horsburgh Lighthouse and labourers for construction of early Singapore defence works. The name 'Klings' was given to Indians. One theory was that the chains of the Indian convicts clanged and the word 'Klings' was derived from their sound. Actually the word 'Kling' referred to Kalinga a place in India. The word 'Kling' was used more than 300 years before the founding of Singapore. The Tamils were referred to as Klings in Portuguese Malacca (1511-1641) and Kampong Kling was already a distinct settlement in Portuguese Malacca and Duch Malacca (1641-1824). The Indian Mutiny of 1857 spread baseless fear in Singapore. In 1867 when the Straits Settlements were transferred from the control of the India Office to that of the Colonial Office the convicts were transferred to the Andaman Islands. Indian convict labour contributed much to the very early development of Singapore.

A few years after the acquisition of Malacca in 1795 another penal settlement was established at the same place. The first batches of prisoners were sent to Malacca from Penang in 1823. Meanwhile Benkoelen was transferred to the Dutch and the convicts stationed there were shifted to Penang. The first batch of convicts on way to Benkoelen were directed to go to Singapore. In 1826, Penang, Malacca and Singapore were incorporated under the Imperial government with Penang as its capital. Later in 1832, the capital was shifted to Singapore. Penal settlement was also opened to

Indian convicts in Arakan and Tennaserim in Burma after the British conquered in 1826. Meanwhile the British authorities in India were seriously discussing the utility of transportation as a reformative measure. British founded a system of labour in which people, whatever their crime, were employed according to their skills as brick makers, carpenters, domestic servants, cattlemen, shepherds and farmers. Educated convicts set the relatively easy work of record- keeping for the convict administration. Women convicts were assumed to be most useful as wives and mothers, and marriage effectively freed a woman convict from her servitude. From 1810, convicts were seen as a source of labour to advance and develop the British colony. Convict labour was used to develop the public facilities of colonies – roads, causeways, bridges, courthouses and hospitals. Convicts also worked for free settlers and small land holders. The discipline of rural labour was seen to be the best chance of reform. This view was adopted by a series of reports for the British government published in 1822-1823. The assignment of convicts to private employers was expanded in 1820s and 1830s, the period when most convicts were sent to the colonies and this became the major form of employment. Convicts formed the majority of the colony's population for the first few decades, and by 1821, there were growing number of freed convicts who were appointed to positions of trust and responsibility as well as being granted land.

The Indian Law Commission of 1837 did not favour the transportation of term-prisoners along with life convicts. While agreeing with the above recommendations the Committee of Prison of Discipline observed "... that the dread of transportation was not regarded as dreadful by the convicts to the same extent as was feared by them some time ago, the Law Commission of 1847 was inclined to restrict the transportation to life-convicts only. Probably, the refusal of many convicts to return to their homes on account of the fear of losing their caste was taken by the Commission to mean that the convicts to some extent did not fear transportation as it was done before. However, the Government of India in decided 1858 to transport, in the first instance convicts sentenced to imprisonment and subsequently for the transportation of convicts sentenced on charges of mutiny, rebellion and for other offences connected therewith. Eventually all convicts under sentence of transportation who for any reason, were not thought expedient to send to the straits settlement or the Tennaserim provinces were to be sent there. Thus, in the beginning it was decided not to send men of desperate or unmanageable character to the Andaman.[11]

In the eyes of many East India Company officials, the sea was central to how convicts experienced the punishment of transportation, for crossing sea or ocean, resulted in a loss of caste. Thus, Indians particularly feared it. Convict responses to transportation were rather more nuanced. Nevertheless, the regulation of convict transportation in the Indian ocean during the period up to 1860, by then the authorities had shipped all Indians and some Burmese convicts to the Andaman islands, which had been re-established as a penal colony in the wake of uprisings that swept across India in 1857-1858. The regulation of Indian convict transportation during the first half of the nineteenth century can be divided into two parts. Before 1834 the East India Company had a monopoly over long distance trade routes, and regularly shipped Indian convicts to Southeast Asia on its Chinese fleet- the 'China Ships'. Those same ships brought convicts back from Southeast Asia to the mainland Indian Jails. After 1834, when the company lost its monopoly, most convicts were transported on such ships and arrangements became somewhat piecemeal and irregular. In general, this lack of regulation only came to light after some incident at sea. One such incident was Runnymade, a convict ship wrecked with lost of life at sea. Some convicts were able to save their life by crossing sea with their ability to swim across the sea. They landed on some of the Andaman Islands where they encountered aboriginals. Most survivers were killed by the aboriginal tribes of Andaman Islands.

Genesis of Andaman Penal Colony

The history of the islands before the eighteenth century is irretrievably shrouded in oblivion and unknown till western colonization. Owing to the ancient course of trade the existence of islands in the midst of Bay of Bengal – Islands was captured by many for years together. The notices of the islands by the old travellers Chinese, Asiatic and European are continuous and they regularly appear in some shape or other on all maps from the "Plotemic" of the fifteenth and sixteenth century, when the East India Company's and Royal Navy Commanders and surveyors began to make accurate reports of parts of the coast in charts preserved in the work of the indefatigable Dalrymple. John Ritchie, who has conducted the Survey of the Bay of Bengal in 1717 to find out the feasibility for navigational and strategic interest. After necessary survey he reported to Warren Hastings, the then Governor-General of India, put it, "in what ever light these islands are considered a thorough knowledge of them will appear to be a matter of great utility". In 1783, Captain Thomas Forest wanted to visit the islands, his purpose being the establishment of some contact with the aboriginals. Five years later Captain Buchanan, who had an opportunity of seeing something of the Coast of Great Andaman, also brought these islands to the notices of East India Company. In a letter dated 19th December 1788, the Governor General Lord Cornwallis, while briefing Lt. Archibald Blair on the object of the survey, stated *inter alia* that, "the material object of the survey is to ascertain in which part of the islands there are good harbours and which it would be most for the company's advantage to project one". It stated among others: 'the primary view of this survey being the organization of a harbour where fleet in the war can refit... may retire in the event of disastrous conflict with an enemy to attain a central position in the Bay...'. On December 20, 1788, Lt. Blair along with Lt. Robert Hyde Colebrook sailed to their destination with two ships namely 'Elizabeth' and 'Viper'. Having completed the survey of the Andaman Island, Lt. Blair submitted the report to the Governor –General to consolidate the Port Cornwallis (Port Blair) in the following words 'it is hardly possible to conceive a more secure and perfect harbour. It is large enough to contain about 50 sailors of the line where they would get perfect shelter from all winds and sea even though there is a seven feet rise in the tide there is no stream to destabilize ships under repair. Its location renders it easy access during monsoon and all the seasons'. Owing to piracies and ill-treatment of ship wrecked and distressed crews, on 12th June' 1789, the Governor–General–Council ordered to colonize the islands. The East India Company through Lord Cornwallis commissioned the great surveyor, Archibald Blair to start a settlement on the ordinary lines. He left Calcutta along with some artificers, labourers and soldiers on 17th September' 1789 and arrived in Port Cornwallis on the 28th, after a voyage which he described as "tedious and tempestuous' during which he lost 'a great part of (his) stocks'. Archibald Blair fixed the camp on his Chatham Island after clearing forests and with no time accommodation for 110 persons was also constructed. A small wooden wharf was also constructed in 1790 to regulate the garrison and ships. On one occasion the ship rangers were sent to Car Nicobar for bringing plants, coconuts, vegetables. They returned with abundance with two Chinese gardeners. The gardeners were soon put to work to boost agricultural product of the Chatham island to sustain itself in times of crisis. The conditions were so good that people were encouraged to bring their families from the mainland. Nonetheless, the success of the settlement in 1789 was undermined, due to strategic reasons the settlement from Chatham island was moved to Port Cornwallis in 1792 (North Andaman). Unprepared for the tropical climate, the convicts proceeded to die by the hundreds. Lacking proper dwellings, they were caught in drenching storms. After the rains, they reeled through the steaming jungles, assaulted by clouds of malaria-bearing mosquitoes. Only 500 of the original 700 survived the first year. It is alleged that 'Kalapani' derived its name from the clouds of black sea water surrounded around the island. No one knows how many convicts fell victim to the aboriginals, but even this horror did not prevent them from trying to escape from the colony. Others were picked clean by Jarawas in the jungle; several were cannibalized by fellow escapees, where they perished miserably in 1796 from the effects of a bad unhealthy site and want of experiences of the climate. Lack of economic returns and the polluting presence of convicts for the indentured labour were factors that contributed to the abolition of transportation to the Andamans. Two views existed on the appearance of penal colonies: (a) from economic point of view, intense labor was required to build the proper settings for the colonies to develop and to reap benefits out of the land. (b) from administrative point of view, newly gained land could serve perfect role as a prison for extremely harsh criminals. With these views combined, the English masters decided to use some of the most distant lands as penal colonies within the Bay of Bengal. They could simply send the most unwanted to these penal colonies to establish settlements and provide labour for the colonial administration. However, the settlement was closed due to large number of deaths within no time and remaining survivors were sent to Bengal. Till 60 years the islands were lying without occupation of British or any other imperialist power.

Re-establishment of Andaman Colony

On November 20, 1857, the Andaman Committee was formed to select the best site for the establishment of the penal settlement. The committee comprised of Dr. F.J. Mouat, Dr. G.R., Playfare ad Lt. Heathcole. After taking stock of the situation the British government recommended to open a full-fledged penal settlement. The Committee was of the opinion that the old Harbour (Lt. Blair, first settlement) was the most ideal place possessing the greater number requisite for a penal settlement. They also suggested changing the name of the old harbour from Port Cornwallis to Port Blair. Accepted by the Governor-General, a decision was taken to establish a penal settlement in the Andaman Islands in January' 1858. Captain Henry Mann, Executive Engineer and Superintendent of Convicts at Moulmein was instructed to hoist the British flag and take the formal possession of the islands consisting of Great and Little Andaman and all the islands adjacent thereto. Henry Mann proceeded to the Andaman on board the 'Semiramis' and hoisted the British Flag with all solemnity on 22 January 1858 to mark respect to Her Majesty the Queen and the East India Company. Initially they cleared the jungles on Chatham and Ross Island for immediate settlement. On March 10, 1858 Dr. James Pettison Walker along with 733 convicts arrived at Chatham Island.[12] A letter dated 16.6.1858 from J.P. Walker, the Superintendent of the Penal settlement of Port Blair to C. Bedon, Secretary to the Government of India shows the following statistics.

In March 1858 Dr. J.P. Walker, an experienced Jail Superintendent arrived with four European officers and 733 convicts cleared Chatham and Ross Islands and started clearing Haddo and Atlantic points. He fixed the headquarters on Ross Island where they have been ever since administered the entire groups of islands till independence of India. He worked under enormous difficulties and with great energy and his inadequate staff was induced in to be very severe. In addition to the natural difficulties of his position he had to contend with constant escapes and attempts at escape and repeated attacks from the Andamanese. On April 1, 1859 about 200 Punjabi convicts organized a plot to murder J.P. Walker for ending British authority in the Andamans. On receipt of prior intimation of the attack of convicts from one of them, Walker's life was saved by two convicts from being shot by a conspirator. All the conspirators were caught and dealt with severe punishment.[13] Meanwhile numbers of steps were taken to improve the conditions of the settlement. However, the deaths were uncontrolled due to bad weather and other water born diseases. After a lapse of a decade again H. Mann took over the charge of settlement and the penal system of the Straits settlement was formally introduced in the Andaman Islands. Around this time H. Mann also started another penal settlement at Nancowry harbour, which virtually lasted for few years and was abandoned in 1872 due to non-performance of the settlement.

The settlement was facing a peculiar problem. Most term convicts were either young or middle age men whose character was different from the criminals. Walker requested the Government of India fair proportion of women in the settlement to stop adulteration and to minimize sex related crimes. With the approval of the Imperial government, Walker appointed two convict family emigration agents at Calcutta and another at North Front Province, presently in Pakistan. Meanwhile the Penal authorities issued notice to the term convicts to call their families and provided a piece of land and other life support items were provided on a small scale. To add some more women folk to the colony the Imperial government instituted a committee to investigate the increasing morality among the convicts at Port Blair. Robert Napier visited the colony and found that out of 8,035 convicts sent to Port Blair since 1858, 2098 had died due to harsh conditions and 612 had deserted due to stringent mental tortures inflicted upon.[14]

The pitiable conditions in the colony cause most deaths. Women were mostly victims and repeatedly raped and molested by the convicts. There was dearth of shelter, clothes and inadequate supply of food grains. Robert Napier considering the hard conditions and difficulties of the settlement stressed immediate need to provide food and cloth and placed request before the Imperial government for construction of 3000 shelters for convicts apart from hospitals, systematic extension of cultivation of fruits and vegetables providing more facilities to married convicts and arrangement of a space of at least 500 cubic feet for each convict. These recommendations were accepted and the gradual improvements were induced in the settlement to promote a self-supporting system. But this system was a complete failure due to alien role of the government. There were no definite rules for the management of convicts. The local crimes were on an upward trend. Finally the government realized the importance of certain rules for the management of convicts on the recommendation of Major Nelson Davis, Secretary of the Chief Commissioner of Burma who visited the settlement in 1867. Ultimately rules of the Governor General in Council for the management of transported convicts under Section 34 of the Act V of 1871 (Prisoners) were passed on July 29, 1874.[15] This Act brought some relief in the crimes at bay.

In 1871, Lord Mayo initiated many important steps to make the colony self-sufficient during extreme weather conditions. On his personal effort, special attention was paid to cultivation, cattle raising, timber and other produces to generate revenue for the requirements of the settlement. The first week of February 1872, witnessed a tragedy which shocked the entire settlement and Imperial government on the mainland. Lord Mayo was killed near Port Blair on visit to colony by Sher Ali, a criminal convict from North-West Frontier Province. After this unusual incident, the colony became a hell for other convicts especially political prisoners. Every convict was suspected and had to undergo severe punishments. Scarlet Campbell, Secretary of Home department inspected the penal colony in 1873. After enough touring he made several suggestions including the improvement the penal system and classification of convicts. On his recommendations to the Governor–General made it clear, "that the main and primary object for which the colony is maintained is to secure that the sentence passed upon convicts is properly carried out under a well regulated system of discipline and to this object the profitable employment of the convicts and the development of the islands must be considered subordinate".[16] He further mentioned in the report that the convicts were no longer afraid of being transported to the Andamans. The convicts regarded Port Blair as a most comfortable place for prisoners. The only drawback was separation from home and its associations.

Sir Henry Norman found that on June 1, 1874, the total convicts in the settlement were 7,820, out of which 895 were female life convicts and 888 term convicts. There were also 500 married couples with 578 children and 1167 tickets of leave convicts, 476 of whom were women. For security reasons Stewart strongly supported the transportation of more term convicts to the penal settlement. Meanwhile Norman suggested that the deplorable moral state of affairs in the settlement were viewed as serious and the same can be improved by introducing marriage among male and female convicts. The tickets of leave convicts may be given more encouragement to call their wives or husbands from the mainland. For the purpose, two agents were recruited. They were Lalla Mundan Singh for Bengal and Lalla Ram Dayal for the North-West Provinces and Oudh, each on a salary of Rupees fifty, with a bonus of rupees two for each female and juvenile member of a family dispatched from Calcutta. Apart from the efforts by the state, the colony also offered and encouraged the convicts to bring their families from mainland India. There were nearly two hundred convicts who were willing to take a chance and made such applications. In order to encourage the scheme, the government went as far as to give sanction to the servants and family members of the convicts to be shipped to the Andamans for a preliminary visit. There were 266 letters dispatched to kins and family members of the convicts. Out of 266 letters, in only two cases the women ultimately travel to Port Blair. Later the officials were confirmed that the families of convicts objected principally on account of caste taboos, as Hindu families hesitated to embark on British ships fearing the loss of caste. The idea of convict family migration was never absolutely abandoned and was taken up once again in 1864 by then the superintendent Major Ford. He saw that convict family emigration scheme as 'very expedient and quite practicable' and felt that it would be the first step to colonization. Indeed many such measures were taken to improve the conditions of the settlement and to give a civilized society status. The officers of the settlement failed to bring convict wives on the pretext of refusal of the convict families to cross the unholy waters. Every effort in this regard went on vain.[17]

Reports about alteration of penal consideration in the settlement attracted the government attention. C.J. Lyall and Major A.S. Lethbridge were sent to Port Blair for ascertaining whether the regulations of the convict management in the Andamans were sufficiently stringent in character for securing the full deterrent effect. They visited Port Blair colony in January 1890. The committee submitted an extensive report in the month of April 1890. In their opinion the convicts preferred transportation to Port Blair than a stay in an Indian jail. Hence the life of a convict in the Andaman should be made more stringent and difficult. In order to make the imprisonment more severe in character, separate confinement for a period of six months after the arrival of the convict at Port Blair should be introduced. In the second spell, the confinement should be in a limited area for two consecutive years would be proper to inflict discipline. Further it desired that the mark system of rewards to convicts should be introduced in the colony to encourage a convict to become a self-supporter in ten years. Both the members emphasized the transportation of more women to the Penal settlement. Indeed their object was to give more facilities to self-supporters to marry female convicts after their term completed. As a result of their recommendations, the authorities in Port Blair enforced strict discipline on the convict brethren. Further, to administer the recommendations very strictly the idea of separate confinement was mooted through making of huge structure called as Cellular Jail, construction was started in the year 1896.

The primary purposes of the incarceration of women in the Andaman Islands had to do with the rehabilitation of male offenders. The very objective was to punish criminalized females and to provide wives for male convicts, as a disincentive to homosexual relationships between men. The women life convicts were similarly dealt with a easier lines. The general principle with regard to them was to divide them into two main classes – those in and those out of the female Jail. Every woman must remain in the female jail, unless in domestic employment by permission or married and living with her husband. Women were eligible for marriage or domestic employment after five years in the colony, and if married they may leave the settlement after 15 years with their husbands, all married couples having to wait; each for the other's full term under the rules, whichever comes last, and they must leave together. If unmarried, women have to remain 20 years in jail. In the jail they rise from class to class and can become petty officers on terms similar to those of men. The term convicts was treated on the same general lines, except that they could not become self-supporters and released at once on the expiry of their sentences. Convict marriages were carefully controlled so as to prevent degeneration into concubance or irregular alliances. The special local Saving Bank proved of great value in inducing a faith on the part of the convicts in the honesty of the government, irrespective of its value in inducing habits of thrift.

In a note written in 1904, W.R.K. Merk regarded it unnecessary and extravagant to spend a considerable amount on a convict by sending him to a penal settlement which had lost its deterrent character and reformative value. Except for a short period in the Cellular Jail, the life of a worst criminal deported to these islands was more comfortable than the life of a less hardened fellow prisoner in an Indian jail. In his opinion the time had come when the transportation to the Andamans should be stopped. But the Government of India did not agree with above opinion of Merk. The total abolition of penal settlement as a place for reception of criminals was not favoured by them. Indeed the government of India regarded the Andaman penal colony as a suitable place of exile for the habitual or especially dangerous offenders. However, they were inclined to reduce the number of convicts in the Andamans by suspending the deportation of male-term prisoners. In order to arrive at a final decision the Government of India referred the matter to the provincial governments for their opinion. On receiving the opinions of the provincial governments, the government of India decided to continue the colony. In 1910, the Imperial Government of India started the transportation of political prisoners to the Andamans.

Meanwhile rejecting all the speculative statements regarding the Andaman penal colony, the Home Secretary after visiting the colony in 1911 said that there was no reason to believe that the punishment of transportation to the Andamans was not fully deterrent in character. Further he admitted that the Andaman system reformed the convict to a great extent. Though capable of improvement, the system was sufficiently punitive. The gross number of the convicts sent to the penal settlement up to year 1901 was 49,592. The persons transported to Port Blair settlement were sent by the Imperial Government of India were murderers, who for some reasons have escaped the death penalty, and the perpetrators of the more heinous offences against the person and property. The sentences they had to undergo were chiefly for life, but a number, varying from a very few to a considerable amount, with long term sentences were also sent from time to time. Except under special circumstances, convicts were received under 18 years of age or over 40 years, nor unless they were mentally fit for hard labour previous to transportation. Youths between 18 and 20 were kept in the boys Gang under special conditions. Girls were occasionally received of 16 or thereabouts, but as all women locally unmarried were kept in the 'Female Jail' in a large enclosure consisting of separate sleeping wards and workshed. There were no special rules for them.

Murder and the heinous offences against the person dacoity, (gang robbery with murder or perpetration of murder) and other heinous offences against property made up nearly the whole total, together accounting for all the other serious offences. The violent character of the convicts was of value to examine. From 1890-1900 the average proportion of convicts who committed or attempted murder was 0.12 per cent, the figures rising to 1.5 per cent in 1894. Neither the nature of the labour nor the discipline enforced appears to have any effect on the tendency to murder, and the motives traced were similar to those disclosed in similar cases among the ordinary population, while murderous assaults were usually committed quite suddenly no opportunity and cause arising. There are also disciplinary gangs all involving degradation either on account of bad character on arrival or while in the settlement. These are known as Cellular Jail prisoners, Viper Island disciplinary, Chatham Island Disciplinary, Chain gang, Habitual criminal gang, and Unnatural crime Gang "D" (for double) ticket men.

Andaman: A Natural Prison

The Great Revolt of 1857 prompted the British authorities to open up a penal colony to execute and impose stringent punishment to nationalists. The British government planned to deport a large number of mutineers to a distant place with the intention to eliminate the intellectuals and brave leaders who actively participated in the revolt. By the first six months of 1858, the British managed to regain their losses in spite of heavy resistance from the prisoners and aboriginals. With the relief of the possibility of British defeat became remote. The British saw themselves as dispensers of divine justice, and given the initial atrocities committed by the mutineers, their cruelties were simply repayment in kind.

Every mutineer was a "black-faced, blood-crazed savage" who did not deserve mercy from the British troops. Their fellow countrymen derided some British like the Governor Lord Canning, who spoke of restraint as "weak" and "indifferent to the sufferings of British subjects". In fact, Canning became known contemptuously as 'clemency Canning'.[17]

The penal transportation has a direct impact on the way political detainees were managed. On this account Allami Fazil Haq 'Khairabadi' inked the political detainees to a slave, and described him "as deprived of liberty, exposed to all the caprice of the family, to whose service he may happen to be assigned, and subject to the most summary laws;" "his condition in no respect differs from that of the slave, except that his master cannot apply corporal punishment by his own hands, or those of his overseer, and has a property in him for a limited period. Idleness and insolence of expression, or of looks, anything betraying the insurgent spirit, subjected him to the chain-gang or the triangle, or hard labour on the roads. "Later British has designated as a slave code, the law which, in that colony, enabled a magistrate, generally himself a master of political detainees, to inflict 50 lashes for disobedience of orders, neglect of work, absconding, abusive language to his master or overseer, or any other disorderly or dishonest conduct." For these offences the political prisoner may likewise be punished by imprisonment, solitary confinement, and labour in irons on the roads. Andaman Island was turned hell on earth and suicide was another way in which the political prisoners responded to his own powerlessness and desperation.

The entire Island was like a jail.[18] In almost perennial rainy weather, with heavy bar fetters and shackles on their feet, surrounded by snakes, leeches and scorpions the freedom fighters were expected, in deep primeval forests to clear a path for roads through marshy land. They were punished and faced hard labour if they slowed down. The British authorities were not contented with banishment alone. They thought of preventing 'contamination' of ideas and thoughts between the men and to enforce strict discipline among the large number of hardened criminals and freedom fighters and there should be more penal preliminary stage of separate confinement for a period of at least 6 months. Accordingly plans to accommodate 600 convicts in separate cells drawn. The cellular jail system in Andamans had definite impact on the Auborn (silence) system that in essence meant associated work by day and separate cells for sleeping in the night to prevent contamination.[19]

At the end of nineteenth century, the construction of the massive structure called the Cellular Jail was undertaken in 1892 as 'matter of great urgency' at a considerable cost. The unique structure of the jail spreading out like a seven-petal flower. In its center it had a tower with a turret. Connected to this were the three storied high seven wings with 698 isolated cells. This is way it is called the Cellular jail. The forbiddingly high walls conjure up fearsome visions and where the Indian freedom fighters underwent unspeakable brutalities for many, many years. The alien government used the Cellular jail to incarcerate anyone who raised his or her voice against the British Empire. Today the Cellular Jail exists in a truncated form but even this is sufficient for anyone to imagine how those who have fought against the British would have suffered. In one respect it is a symbol of the cruelty of the British imperialism, while in another it is a symbol of the sacrifices for the cause of independence.[20]

In the beginning of the twentieth century the press and public in India expressed their resentment on reports of the cruel treatment to political detainees in the 'Kala Pani'. Demands for the abolition of the colony was continuously made by political leaders in their writings and speeches. In November 1913, Sir. Reginald Craddock, the Home member, visited the Andaman penal settlement to study the situation personally. In his lengthy report he mentioned that the penal system in Andamans appeared to be perfect in theory. According to him, the terror of crossing the 'Kala Pani' was now an exploded *bogey* to Indians who were voluntarily going to distant places like Fiji and Columbia. The existence of immorality among the prisoners on a wide scale on account of shortage of women in the settlement was deplored by him. In these circumstances he suggested following three alternatives:

- To abolish the Andaman penal settlement;
- To remedy only the serious defects of the system in order to make it less harmful ; and
- To reform the entire penal system of India including the existing system of the Andamans.[21]

Meanwhile the Indian Jails committee made a remarkable statement stating that the existing system in the Andamans was regarded undesirable to them even if increased staff was provided to the administration of the penal settlement. In their opinion the Andaman penal system had lost its deterrent effect, involved enormous expenditure and exposed prisoners to adverse climate conditions. The committee did not regard the self-supporter system a success, mainly due to paucity of women in the settlement. Instead of retaining Andaman as a place of deportation for a larger number of prisoners only.

Keeping the worst conditions and press and public criticism in general to the penal system in Andamans, Sir William Vincent, Home Secretary to the Government of India announced the abolition of the penal settlement and arrange a speedy return of prisoners to the Indian jails. Further he issued orders that the repatriation of the prisoners from Andaman would be gradual because the local governments were not in a position to accommodate about twelve to fifteen thousand prisoners in a short period. Based on the recommendations of Jails Committee, punishment of solitary confinement and chain gang were abolished. Flogging was rare. No convicts outside the jail were kept in fetters. Facilities for outdoor games and library were provided during leisure time. Some more steps were taken to improve the conditions of the penal system in Andamans and few unmarried female convicts were repatriated to their native places.

Meanwhile the number of prisoners were overcrowded in the several provincial jails and the local governments expressed their inability to accommodate such an unexpected demand due to large scale political agitation. This period was crucial for the British authorities to reconsider the reopening of the Andaman penal system temporarily. Keeping aside all the criticism, the Deputy Secretary Gwynne laid great stress on the development of the resources of the islands and indeed he observed that there was no alternative but to reopen temporarily the deportation of the prisoners.

Sir Alexander Muddiman, the Home Member visited the islands in November 25, 1925 and recommended the penal settlement to be continued because he felt that:

- There was lack of accommodation in the jails of several provinces of India for prisoners repatriated from the Andamans;
- If the penal settlement of Port Blair is abandoned the whole administration of the island would collapse;
- The closing of the settlement would adversely affect about three thousand self–supporters in the islands who were living in a state of semi-independence; and
- The strategic location of these islands in the Bay of Bengal was another important reason and the immense natural wealth of these islands, which would be developed into valuable assets, prevented the British government to abandon the settlement.[22]

The Government of India further certified that the reduction of convict population in the settlement considerably hampered the progress of the development programmes of the islands. On account of shortage of labourers in the islands several plans could not be executed. In order to promote self-supporters and free population, the Government of India extended grants of land on lease for fifty years to attract more people from the mainland. To strengthen the settlement, the Government of India declared plans for the development of forest and agriculture in the islands to make semi self-sufficient penal system. This policy of developing the islands through the agency of an enlarged population of ex-convicts and their families was followed by the British government till the occupation of the Japanese in 1942. The islands were reoccupied by the British in 1945 and indeed they granted general pardon to all the convicts and self-supporters. Finally the Government of India abolished the penal settlement in 1945.[23]

Infamous name 'Kalapani'

The Andaman islands were more recognizable as 'Kala Pani', but the exact reason for giving this infamous name to the islands is still in the dark. The local born view that the colour of sea waters of these islands was black either in itself or because of the reflection of the thick and dark black clouds, which almost always remained overcast. There are others who say that the stone of the hills surrounding the sea was black which by its reflection made the colour of the sea appear black. However, numerous scholars reject this theory, and according to them the expression 'Kala Pani' has been used with reference to the Sanskrit word 'Kal', which means time or death. The word 'Kala Pani' thus, meant the water of death or a place of death from where only the luckiest returned."[24] The British, immediately after the establishment of penal settlement in the Andaman in 1858, also referred these islands as existing across the 'Black Water'. Aden, an island in the Arabian Sea where Vasudeo Balwant Phadke was transported, too, was called 'Kala Pani'.

Obviously, therefore, the name 'Kala Pani' was given to these penal settlements, which were far removed from the mainland of the country by long stretch of seawaters where hardcore criminals were to be transported from the country. The jail authorities there were at liberty, rather, were instructed by the British government to treat the prisoners with extreme unkindness and from where only the luckiest could return. 'Kala Pani' or 'Black Water' virtually meant cruel and ruthless treatment to the prisoners till death. A sentence of deportation to 'Kala Pani' meant a warrant for throwing the prisoner in living hell to face heard or unheard trials and tribulations and to lead a life of a beast or even worse than that. Expatriation to 'Kala Pani' for life was worse than death penalty. The Indian revolutionaries were doomed to 'Kala Pani' to undergo these harsh punishments but they in turn immortalized these islands by their selfless sacrifices. Although the Andaman and Nicobar Islands are among the world's most beautiful islands and neither the soil, nor the water of these islands is black, but the British government had created a situation to call these islands as 'Kala Pani' because of the inhuman barbarisms inflicted on the patriot prisoners fighting for the liberation of their motherland who were transported from the mainland and gaoled in these islands. The term "Kala Pani" is interwoven with the trials and tribulations faced by the brave political prisoners in Cellular Jail and of those freedom fighters of the first war of independence who were brought to this island to lead a "hell like life".[25]

REFERENCES

1. *Encyclopaedia of America*, Grotier, Danbury, 1984, p. 619.
2. Aparna Vaidik, Settling the Convicts: Matrimony and Domesticity in the Andamans, *Studies in History*, Vol. XVII, No. 2, New Delhi, July- December, 2006. p. 220.
3. Bhattacharya. Dr B.K., *Prisons* (1958).
4. Tapas Kumar Banerji: *Background to Indian Criminal Law* (1963).

5. Mathur. L.P., *Kalapani*, Eastern Book Corporation, Delhi, 1985, p. 73.
6. *Ibid.*, p. 37.
7. Mukerjee. Dr. S.K, *Islands of India*, Ministry of I & B, GOI, New Delhi, 1992, pp. 133-140.
8. In 1890, a two member committee consisting of Sir. C J Lyall and Dr. A.S. Lethbridge specially recommended that the convicts in the Andamans should be confined in separate cells in a limited area to cut off all means of communication between the prisoners – based on the 'Model Prison' or infamous 'Pentonville Prison' in England. *Encyclopedia of Americana*, Grolier, Danbury, 1984. pp. 619- 623.
9. Standing at the seacoast in the northeastern part of the Port Blair, the Cellular Jail has a unique architecture. In its original form, it had seven wings, much like the spokes of a bicycle. A three-storied structure, it had 698 cells and no dormitories. The central tower was used by it sentries to keep watch and control the cells. Built with bricks brought from Myanmar, the jail was constructed during 1896-1906 at a cost of Rs. 5,17,352. The purpose of the jail was to condemn the largest number of revolutionary elements to long terms of imprisonment at the minimum cost. It was designed that the front of each wing faced the back of the other. Each cell measuring 13 and a half feet by 7 and a half feet had an iron grill door well secured with sturdy iron bolt and lock on the rectangular groove on the outside of the cell wall and also a few inches away from the entrance door making it impossible to reach it from within (Mukerjee. Dr. S.K., *Islands of India*, Ministry of I & B, GOI, New Delhi, 1992. pp. 133-140)
10. Clare Anderson, *Convicts in the Indian Ocean: Transportation from South Asia to Mauritius, 1815-1853*, Macmillan Press, London, 2000. p. 162.
11. Home Department, Judicial Branch, Original Consultation 21 January 15, 1858, No. 21, National Archives of India, New Delhi.
12. The settlement on Chatham Island flourished under Archibald Blair, but unfortunately on the advice of Commodore Cornwallis, brother of the Governor –General, the site was changed for strategic reasons to North-East harbour, but the settlement faced misery from sickness. Finally the settlement was abandoned in 1796, on account of mass sickness. It contained 270 convicts and 550 free Bengali settlers. The convicts

were transferred to Penang and the settlers taken to Bengal. After that the islands remained unoccupied by the colonial rulers till 1858.

13. Home Department, Judicial Branch, Port Blair, A proceedings July 29, 1859. No. 32, National Archives of India, New Delhi.
14. Later the deserted convicts were presumed as dead. Ibid. Home Department, No. 32.
15. Mathur. L.P. *Kalapani*, Eastern Book Corporation, Delhi, 1985. p. 40.
16. Home Department, Port Blair Branch, A proceedings, February 1873, No. 1, NAI, New Delhi.
17. Home Judicial (30 November 1860) National Archives of India, New Delhi. pp. 37-38.
18. Aparna Vaidik, Settling the Convict: Matrimony and Domesticity in the Andamans, *Studies in history*, Vol. XXII, No. 02, July- December 2006, Sage Publications, New Delhi. pp. 221-251.
19. Satadru Sen, The female Jails of colonial India, *The Indian Economic and Social History Review*, 396, 4 (2002), Sage Publications, New Delhi. p. 418.
20. The British occupied these islands in the year 1773. Since then the islands were established as Penal colony and converted into a natural Jail after 1857 revolt. Majumder. R.C., (1975) Penal Settlement in Andamans, *Gazetteers, Government of India*, New Delhi. pp. 65-67.
21. In 1890, a two member committee consisting of Sir. C J Lyall and Dr. A.S. Lethbridge specially recommended that the convicts in the Andamans should be confined in separate cells in a limited area to cut off all means of communication between the prisoners–based on the 'Model Prison' or infamous 'Pentonville Prison' in England. *Encyclopedia of America*, Grotier incorporated, Danbury, 1984. pp. 618-623.
22. Standing at the seacoast in the northeastern part of the Port Blair, the Cellular Jail has a unique architecture. In its original form, it had seven wings, much like the spokes of a bicycle. A three-storied structure, it had 698 cells and no dormitories. The central tower was used by it sentries to keep watch and control the cells. Built with bricks brought from Myanmar, the jail was constructed during 1896-1906 at a cost of Rs. 5,17,352. The purpose of the jail was to condemn the largest number of

revolutionary elements to long terms of imprisonment at the minimum cost. It was designed that the front of each wing faced the back of the other. Each cell measuring 13 and a half feet by 7 and a half feet had an iron grill door well secured with sturdy iron bolt and lock on the rectangular groove on the outside of the cell wall and also a few inches away from the entrance door making it impossible to reach it from within. Mukherji. Dr. S.K., *Islands of India*, Ministry of I & B, GOI, New Delhi, 1992. p. 135.

23. Iqbal Narain, The Andaman Story, Vikas Publications, New Delhi, 1978. p. 193.
24. Home Department, Port Blair Branch, A proceedings, February 1873 No. 1, National Archives of India, New Delhi. pp. 41-43
25. Home Department, Andaman Branch, Jails, File No. 20/26, July 1922, National Archives of India, New Delhi. pp. 45-46.

2
Andaman Penal Order : Inside Story

This chapter critically surveys the growth of Penal colony in Andaman Island from the middle of the nineteenth century till the attainment of Indian independence. The focus is on the politics of colonialism and effects of imperialism which was the dominant note of this chapter. The object is to present a thematic treatment of the subject covering the Penal Order and its impact on political prisoners and convicts especially revolutionaries. Indeed the present study of penal system deals with exclusive role of British in bringing the correctional system by enforcing strict discipline in the form of torture, intimidation and political expulsion. Every political prisoner was a "black-faced, blood-crazed savage" who did not deserve mercy from the British was the policy of imperalist. A large number of political prisoners were hanged. Widespread looting of Indian property, religious or secular, was common and endorsed. Later, convicted mutineers were lashed to the muzzles of cannon and had a round shot fired through their body. This was a cruel punishment intended to blow the body into pieces, thus depriving the victim of any hope of entering paradise. Indians called this punishment "the devil's wind".

In colonial India, the British had made various penal colonies. In the early days of settlement, Singapore was the recipient of Indian convicts, who were tasked with clearing the jungles for settlement and early public works. Mostly, penal colony served its purpose as a prison for political offenders; therefore the environment was not hospitable, which was a means to slowly kill them (It is not strange to think that any government would not like political offenders, who have ideology different from that of the conventional government). In the Imperialistic Period, many European countries including Britain established penal colonies among their frontier territories. Infact, these penal colonies served various purposes for the European mother nations. First of all, they could serve an excellent prison for criminals, because there was no away to escape if the island was in a distant place. Moreover, since the imprisoned sometimes did not have a lifetime sentence, distant penal colonies delayed their possible return to the motherland governments. Secondly, penal colonies could be easily developed with the help of penal labour. Usually, severe and harsh criminals were transported to penal colonies to do forced labour. To pay the price for their crimes, the offenders had to suffer additional punishment other than just the depravation of liberty. The penal labour could temporarily replace the need for labour before sufficient number of immigrants were available. This was rather critical labour resource for the colony administrations, so some poor people were charged with penal sentence for creating just minor crimes. Lastly, the penal colonies were places for religious minorities. When the government persecuted certain religious minorities, either the persecuted chose to go to the penal colonies to enjoy the freedom of religion, or the government forced them to go to penal colonies, where obligation to protect the people was not held. Infact, a slave code enables the penal masters, generally a master of prisoners, to inflict 50 lashes for drunkenness, disobedience of orders, neglect of work, absconding, abusive language to his master or overseer, or any other disorderly or dishonest conduct. For these offences the prisoners may likewise be punished by imprisonment, solitary confinement, and labour in irons on the roads.

Nonetheless, penal concerns were secondary to economic ones, not much emphasis was put on strict discipline, surveillance and segregation. Most penal colonies were turned to hell on earth and suicide was another way in which the prisoners responded to his own powerlessness and desperation. Andaman penal system was too harsh, inhuman and known for its stringent banishment. Veer Savarkar aptly compared the treatment of prisoner to a slave, and described him 'as deprived of liberty, exposed to all the caprice of the family, to whose service he may happen to be assigned, and subject to the most summary laws, his condition in no respect differs from that of the slave, except that his master cannot apply corporal punishment by his own hands, or those of his overseer, and has a property in him for a limited period. Idleness and insolence of expression, or of looks, anything betraying the insurgent spirit, subject him to the chain gang or the triangle, or hard labour on the roads.' A penal colony is a settlement used to detain prisoners and generally use them for penal labour in an economically underdeveloped part of the state's (usually colonial) territories, and on a far larger scale than a prison farm. The most well known in the Indian sub-continent was Andaman Islands and Hijli. British Empire used these colonies as such for more than 90 years. The prison regime was often harsh, sometimes including severe physical punishment, so even if prisoners were not sentenced for the rest of their natural lives, many died from hunger, disease, medical neglect, excessive labour, or during an escape attempt. In the penal colony system, prisoners were sent far away to prevent escape and to discourage returning after their sentence expired. Penal Colonies were often located in frontier lands, especially the more inhospitable parts, where their unpaid labour could benefit the metropoles before immigration labour became available, or even afterwards where they are much cheaper; in fact sometimes people (especially the convicts, following a similar social logic as could see them domestically employed) were sentenced for trivial or dubious offenses to generate cheap labour.

The Great Revolt of 1857 prompted the British authorities to consider opening up a penal colony to impose stringent punishment to hardcore nationalist and isolating the political intellectuals across South Asia. The British created penal order in Andaman to set within the rhetoric of moral reform, which entailed distancing the political convict from his familiar surroundings and subjecting him to hard labour. There existed inherent contradictions within this rhetoric of reform that illustrated the conflict that existed between the penal and economic aims of transportation. The penal transportation has a direct impact on the way political prisoners were managed.

Reading the history of transportation from the perspective of Indian Penal system and law-making can perhaps provide a deeper understanding of the ideological role that each punishment played. Penal transportation, besides its utility as developing and colonizing far-flung colonies, served an ideological function for the British. A substitute for capital punishment, penal transportation was intended to impart a benign and merciful appearance to colonial authoritarianism and at the same time was used for dealing with problems of collective crime. This punishment was resurrected and deployed whenever the colonial order felt threatened by a popular upsurge or a collective resistance by the colonized people. Early in the first decade of the 18th century, the roots of the East India Company were firmly entrenched in India. The British were subjecting Indians to a lot of abject atrocities, snatching away land from peasants, destroying the livelihood of craftsmen, increasing taxes, usurping the states from the Nawabs and native kings. Ordinary people, soldiers, nawabs and kings were all being terrified and harassed. Generally everywhere there was resentment and revolt. People were determined to do away with the East India Company. In the 1780s, 1820s and the post-1857 periods when penal transportation was extensively resorted to by British, were also periods of the rise of banditry, thuggee and popular rebellions in the Indian sub-continent. What lends credence to this supposition is that most of the convicts sent to Mauritius and the Andamans were convicted of dacoity, murder and banditry. The character of colonies having convict stations or employing labour on a particular scale was different from that of settler colonies. It is really the use of a colony particularly for penal purposes, as a prison, which qualified it as a penal settlement. The colonization of most of the overseas and far-flung colonies began with the use of penal labour, because most of them required a certain amount of resources and labour input in order to make them habitable by European standards. The actual character of the settlement was decided only after they were developed, depending on the strategic, economic and political needs of the colonial state. As a result many colonies like Andaman became convict settlements.

The British started the system of the transportation of Indian prisoners through an overseas penal settlement in 1787. They used the punishment of transportation, and during the same period shipped a small number of offenders to foreign jails across South Asia. A sizeable number of prisoners were kept in some of India's largest jails, Alipur near Calcutta, as well as in smaller district jails across the Bombay and Madras presidencies. Transportation emptied overcrowded Indian prisons and assured new company settlements as a supply of cheap labour. In fact, the convict workforce was vital to the development of early colonial infrastructure. The East India Company established its first penal settlement for the reception of Indian convicts in Benkulu (1787 - 1825). The Andaman Islands (1793-96), Penang otherwise known as Prince of Wales Island (1790-1860), Melaka and Singapore (1825-60) and the Burmese provinces of Arakan and Tenasserim (1828-62) followed soon after. First time a larger number of Bengal prisoners convicted for various crimes were sent to Benkoelen penal settlement in Sumatra. Later on prisoners from Madras and other provinces were also sent to establish settlement. According to Sir Thomas Stamford Raffles, Governor of Sumatra, the object of transporting convicts to a far off place was to reclaim them from bad habits but he pointed out in a letter written to the Government of India that in the system prevailing in the penal colony at the time the above objectives were not achieved. In his opinion even those prisoners who expressed an inclination to reform themselves, were not given sufficient encouragement. Infact the main cause of the failure of the authorities in achieving the desired results was in employing the convicts in the task of clearing forests, making roads and for developing the settlement at Singapore, Penang, Malacca, Tennaserim and Aracan and the Andamans.

For this the first penal colony in Andaman was established for convicts in the year 1792 and lasted up to 1796. From 1792, the colony of Andamans was officially a penal colony, comprised mainly of convicts, mariners and the wives of the marines. This was possible due to John Ritche, who had the conducted survey of the Bay of Bengal in 1717, who stated, "in whatever light these islands are considered, a thorough knowledge of them will appear to be matter of great utility". He was reporting to Warren Hastings, the then Governor General of India. In 1783, Captain Thomas Forrest wanted to visit the islands for his purpose being the establishment of some contact with the aboriginals. Five years later Captain Buchanan, who had an opportunity of seeing something of the Coast of Great Andaman also brought these islands to the notices of the East India Company. In a letter dated 19th December '1788, the then Governor General of India, Lord Cornwallis, while briefing Lt. Blair on the object of the survey, stated inter alia that, "the material object of the survey is to ascertain in which part of the islands there are good harbours and where it would be best for the company's advantage to project one". On June 12, 1789, the Governor-General decided to colonize the islands for dual interest, one, being to provide safe anchorage to distressed ships during the cyclones and other natural calamities to international shipping lines and the second to check the sea-pirates and to provide shelter to ship-wreck crews. Meanwhile, Lt. Blair left Calcutta along with some artificers, labourers and soldiers on September 17, 1789 and arrived in Port Cornwallis on September 28, 1789, after a voyage which he described and "tedious and tempestuous" during which he lost 'a great part of his stock'. Indeed, the Andaman Island was the site of the first penal colony in the Indian subcontinent and was established in 1792 to transport the hard-core criminals who have been awarded stringent punishment by the British courts. Thus opened a remarkable chapter in the darkest pages of Indian colonial history as a 'Kalapani', which recollects the hardest possible discipline short of death a 'hellish inferno'. But this colony proved to be very dangerous because many convicts either died due to malaria or due to incriminating climate, which later abandoned in 1796. No one knows how many convicts fell victim to the aboriginals of Andaman Islands, but even this horror did not prevent them from trying to swim the vast blue waters. Others were picked clean by scavengers in the jungle; several were cannibalized by fellow escapees. What a place this must have been to drive men to such desperate feats! Yet Andaman Island, like the Devil Island, iniquitous and dismal in itself, gave rise to some of the great epics of human courage and fortitude. Without awful conditions in the colony. Most of the atrocities of Andaman Island took place in the process of cleaning jungles. The prisoners were forced to work in long spells, assaulted by malarial mosquitoes and baked by the sun. They were underfed and overworked. Their daily work task was to cut one cubic meter wood. Failure to meet the quota resulted in their being fed only dry bread that day. The next day the prisoner was confronted with the same quota he'd been unable to meet the day before. There is always a certain type of individual who chooses not to die like a lamb. The brutal camps were not only scenes of degradation and despair, but also arenas for acts of extraordinary courage. Although the convicts in the punishment camps were made to work naked except for shoes, there are cases on record of men running into the jungle, unarmed. In spite of fantastic odds, such escapes occasionally succeeded. The penalty for failing to escape was horrific. Three attempts to escape resulted in a classification of "Incorrigible." After completing their formal punishment in solitary, such "incos" were banished to the most dreaded camps where they worked like beasts all day; at night, they were placed in irons until the following morning. Mount Harriet was the deadliest camp in the colony, a large number of convicts died due to inhospitable conditions. There was only one way to escape by sea; through hundreds of miles of swim across to reach any land nearest to colony. To escape by sea required a slender Indian dugout canoe, provisions, a comrade with naval experience and the direct intervention of God. Hoping to better understand the attempt to escape from Andaman Island by sea, almost always without navigational instruments, or, for that matter, a navigator who could use the instruments should they be available.

Escape from Andaman Island seems to appeal to the primordial instincts of people everywhere who, though socialized and communized, inherently regret the loss of individuality that accompanies the socializing process. We know that thousands of men perished in the Bay of Bengal trying to escape from Andaman Island in a canoe. They died of thirst, dysentery, hunger; they died in storms that swamped their fragile crafts; they died beneath the knives of sun-maddened comrades. To sail east along the coast Burma required 10 days of constant exposure to the elements, tossed by the seas, drenched in storms, boiled by the sun. The British had planned to send them far away to prevent escape and to discourage returning after their sentence expired. Penal Colonies were often located in frontier lands, especially the more inhospitable parts like Andaman, where their unpaid labour could benefit the metropolis. In such a society, the concepts like democracy and liberalism at first had no place. The early years were increasingly desperate ones as the colony struggled to establish and feed itself. The prison system in Andaman was often harsh, sometimes including severe physical punishment, so even if prisoners were not sentenced for the rest of their natural lives, many died from hunger, disease, medical neglect, excessive labour, or during an escape attempt. "Of this Penal colony, it was reported thirty years later that the convicts rarely desired to return to their country. They were encouraged to marry, formed connections in the place and found so many inducements to remain there that they practically became colonists." "Indian convicts sent to Singapore Penal Settlement were under no restraint and received no support and were allowed to provide for themselves. They differed in no respect from free population of the place, excepting that they had to give security for appearance whenever required."[1]

The British used Andaman Islands as a penal colony both in terms and the usual sense through the system of indentured servitude. Most notably, the Chatam Islands were originally designed as a penal colony. Prisoners would be transported by out boats to plantation upon arrival in the colony. It is generously estimated that some 200 prisoners were sent everyday to Chatam Islands to clear jungles and laying of roads in surrounding areas. The entire Andaman Island was like a jail. In almost perennial rainy weather, with heavy bar fetters and shackles on their feet, surrounded by snakes, leeches and scorpions the freedom fighters were expected, in deep primeval forests to clear a path for roads through marshy land. About Andaman Penal Settlement, Banerji quoting a letter dated 8th February, 1856 of Captain Henry Hopkinson, Governor of Arakan States: "Prisoners at first would have to be employed in making the station with its roads, barracks, public buildings and jails and when completed, those who had not forfeited the privilege by misconduct would receive ticket of leave and be allowed to labour for their own property." They were punished and faced hard labour if they slowed down work due to heavy handedness. The British authorities were not contented with banishment alone. They thought of preventing 'contamination' of ideas and thoughts between the men and to enforce strict discipline among the large number of hardened criminals and freedom fighters and there should be more penal preliminary stage of separate confinement for a period of at least 6 months. Accordingly plans to accommodate 600 convicts in separate cells were drawn. The cellular jail system in Andamans had definite impact on the Auborn (silence) system that in essence meant associated work by day and separate cells for sleeping in the night to prevent contamination. Convicts were given sentences of seven years, fourteen years or life. However, none of them were allowed to return to India, on pain of death. Transportation to Andaman effectively came to an end on re-occupation of British in 1945.

The Andaman Penal system was sui-generic. It has grown up on its own lines and was been gradually adapted to the requirements of penal character. This system has also been independent and was never at any time based on the inside prison system and has been continuously under development till it was abolished. Indeed the fundamental principle was on which the penal system was founded was to bring reformative changes among the criminals particularly the hard core criminals and dacoits. The success of the colonial enterprise in the Andaman Islands rested on transforming the transported prisoners into a law-abiding and gainfully employed citizens of the British empire and converting the islands space into a flourishing agricultural colony. The penal settlement in Andamans were almost like a natural prison, but it was different from the modern prison system. The penal settlement in Andaman was a place for the detention of a certain class of prisoners only viz., transported convicts. The Andaman system of penal settlement was practically worked on rules contained in the Andaman and Nicobar Manual consisting of two parts:

- Rules and Orders issued under legal authority, and
- Administrative and executive orders passed by the Imperial Legislature.

The system has always rested on the Indian prisoners Act 1876 and the Andaman and Nicobar Regulation. The rules or orders having legal authority in the Andaman and Nicobar manual and they stand are:

- Rules of Governor-General-in-Council for the management of transported convicts, under Section 34 of Act V of 1871 (Prisoners hearing dated July 29, 1874) and since modified by many orders of the Government of India.
- Subsidiary rules of the Chief commissioner with the sanction of the Governor – general in Council, under section 18 of the Andaman and Nicobar regulation 174, dated December 4, 1874 and continued under section 33, Andaman and Nicobar regulation, III of 1876.
- Bye-laws of the Superintendent (section 32 (b) Andaman and Nicobar regulation, III of 1876 and rule VI (7) of the Governor–General in council's rules for transported convicts 1874). These bye-laws are knowing settlement standing orders, and are included in the Manual and the Prisoners Act III of 1900, and though no rule – making power is conferred by the new act in this connection the existing rules of governor – general in council and the bye–laws referred to therein are enforce under the general clauses act X of 1897, section 24.[2]

Indeed the major principles of penal settlement in Andamans are as follows:

- the prisoners were defined as in the power of the government that held him, rather than of the individuals who were his immediate captors;
- the British government was responsible for the safety, humane treatment, food, quarter, clothing of prisoners with the standards of well- being;
- the prisoners were to be insulated included guarantees against their exploitation by the captor, while allowing for their secure detention or their parole under obligation not to reassume arms; and

- finally the government included providing the identification of them and assigned the prisoners certain duties and their rank and abiding by inter-law and rules for their detention established by the captor power.[3]

Penal System

The Andaman Islands were established in 1858 as a penal colony. After the first War of Indian Independence of 1857, at that time there was social upheaval with the beginnings of massive agricultural, industrial and social change, the government was faced with overcrowded prisons and prison ships and no suitable destination to transport their convicts. Blair's discovery and annexation of Andaman Islands on the east coast of India in 1858, aroused new interest. In particular, Dr. F.J. Mouat, Dr. G.R. Playfare ad Lt. Heathcole after taking the stock of the situation recommended the British government to open a full-fledged penal settlement and convict colony. For this and for related strategic and commercial reasons, the British government decided to embark on the new settlement project. The first settlement consisted of about 733 convicts and their Marine guards and officers, led by Dr. J.P. Walker arrived at Ross Islannd in the first fleet of 'Semiramis' transport ships accompanied by 2 small warships, in March, 1858. Finding the area unsuitable for keeping convicts, they actually settled at Port Blair Harbour as it is better known as Port Blair Island on March 1858, the day is now celebrated as "Andaman Day".

In such a society, the emerging Imperalism had no concept of democracy and liberalism at first instance. The early years were increasingly desperate ones as the colony struggled to establish and feed itself. By 1892, the first signs of stability were appearing but Governor Phillip, weakened by illness and the deprivations of those years, returned to England, leaving the colony in the hands of military

Lieutenant-Governors. Until 1874, the military governors were absolute rulers, the only power superior to them being the British Parliament at Westminster in England, nearly, 600 miles away by sea. The governors' rights were granted to them under an Act of the British Parliament of 1787, which gave them their commissions and instructions, but the distance and the infrequency of communication with the rest of the world meant that governors often exercised far wider powers than they had been given. While governors retained virtually absolute authority, a great deal of effective power in the colony lay with the military, in particular the officers of the Corps raised especially for duty in the colony from 1858 on. The officers quickly gained significant land holdings and monopoly control over trade, especially of rum and alcohol imports. The arrival of the first free settlers in 1858 was the first sign of a need for change. The number of free settlers and merchants steadily grew, as did the number of native born people and prisoners who had served their time and were free citizens. And, as the size and importance of the free citizenry grew in relation to that of the prisoners and military, so, inevitably, would also grow a demand for democratic change.

The full penal systems as prevailed in the Andamans were as follows:

- The life prisoners are received into the Andaman Island for six months, where the discipline is of the severest but the work is not hard. They are then transferred to the associated jail for 18 months, where the work was hard but the discipline less irksome. For the next three years the life under supervision. For his labour he receives no reward, but his capabilities are studied. During the next five years he remains a labouring convict but was eligible for the petty posts of supervision and the basic wage to save in the special saving bank. At this time he may have completed

10 years in transportation and can receive a ticket-of-leave (self-supporters). In this condition he earns his own living in a village. He can farm kept cattle, and marry or send for his family. But he is not free, has no civil rights and cannot leave the settlement or be idle. After 20 – 25 years spent in the settlement with approved conduct he may be absolutely released. While a self-supporter, he is at first assisted with house, food and tools and pays no taxes or cesses, but after three to four years, according to certain conditions, he receives no assistance and was charged with every public payment which could be demanded of him as a free man.

- The women life prisoners were similarly dealt with but on altogether easier lines. The general principle with regard to them was to divide them into two main classes: - those in and those out of the female jail. Every woman must remain in the female jail for a period of six months, unless in domestic employ by permission or married and living with her husband. Women were eligible for mission of marriage or domestic employ after five years in the settlement and if married they may leave the settlement after 15 years with their husbands. All married couples having to wait each for other's full term under the rules, which comes last and they must leave together. If unmarried women have to remain 20 years. Up the jail they rise from clans to class and can become petty officers on terms similar to those of the men.

- Term convicts are treated on the same general lines, except that they cannot become self-supporters and are released at once on the expiry of their sentences; and

- Convict marriages are carefully controlled so as to prevent degeneration into concubinage or irregular alliances and special local saving bank has proved of great value in inducing a faith on the part of the

> convicts in the honesty of the government, irrespective of its value in deducing habits of thrift and diminishing the temptation to revenue or the sake of money boarding privately.[4]

Convict labour

Governor Philip (1788-1792) founded a system of labour in which people, whatever their crime, were employed according to their skills - as brick makers, carpenters, nurses, servants, cattlemen, shepherds and farmers. Educated convicts were set to the relatively easy work of record-keeping for the convict administration. Women convicts were assumed to be most useful as wives and mothers, and marriage effectively freed a woman convict from her servitude. From 1858, convicts were seen as a source of labour to advance and develop the British colony. Convict labour was used to develop the public facilities of the colonies-roads, causeways, bridges, courthouses and hospitals. Convicts also worked for free settlers and small land holders. The discipline of rural labour was seen to be the best chance of reform. This view was adopted by Superintendent in a series of reports between 1858-72. The assignment of convicts to private employers was expanded in the 1820s and 1830s, the period when most convicts were sent to the colonies, and this became the major form of employment. Convicts formed the majority of the colony's population for the first few decades, and by 1901 there was a growing number of freed convicts who were appointed to positions of trust and responsibility as well as being granted land.

The Convict Experience

In the mid-1860s only around six per cent of the convict population were 'locked up', the majority were working for free settlers and the authorities around the Islands. Even so, convicts were often subject to cruelties such as leg-irons and the lash. Convicts sometimes shared deplorable conditions. One convict described the working thus: 'We have to work from 14-18 hours a day. The experience of those convicts is recorded in the *Faizal Haq Kariabadi* written by convicts. In addition to the physical demands of convict life, some convicts arrived without sufficient English knowledge to communicate easily with others. By 1858, about 700 of the convicts had been sentenced in Andaman Islands. Many who were sent there could only speak Urdu and vernaculars, so as well as being exiled to a strange country they were unable to speak with most of their fellow convicts.

Most of the prisoners were mutineers who had been convicted in the great cities of Indian Sub-continent. Only the those sentenced in jails within India were likely to have been convicted of rural crimes. Transportation was an integral part of the British system of punishment. It was a way to deal with increased poverty and the severity of the sentences for larceny. Simple larceny, or robbery, could mean transportation for seven years. Waging voice against the state could mean death by hanging. Men had usually been before the courts a few times before being transported, whereas women were more likely to be transported for a first offence. The great majority of convicts were working men and women with a range of skills.

In the mid-1860s only around six per cent of the convict population were 'locked up', the majority working for free settlers and the authorities around the island. Even so, prisoners were often subject to cruelties such as leg-irons and the lash. Places like Viper Island and North Bay were well known for this kind of punshiment being executed to most notorious convicts. Prisoners sometimes shared deplorable conditions. One convict described the working thus: 'We have to work from 14-18 hours a day, sometimes up to late evening, The inhuman driver struck one, Mirza Khan, with a heavy thong.' The experience of these convicts is recorded by Veer Savarkar, in his book *'My deportation to Andaman'* were often sad or critical. In addition to the physical demands of convict life, some convicts arrived without sufficient English to communicate easily with others. By 1860, about 1,800 of the convicts had been sentenced in Chatham Island. Many who were sent there could only speak Hindi, Urdu, Panjabi and few others Bengali, so alongwith being exiled to a strange country they were unable to to with most of their fellow convicts.

Classification of Convicts

The convicts while in the settlement are divided into several categories. The great economic division for both sexes was the labouring convicts and self-supporters. The former perform all the labour, skilled and unskilled and the later are chiefly engaged in agriculture and food supplies. The Commissariat Division was into rationed and not rationed. In the former class are nearly all the labouring convicts and in the latter all the self-supporters are some of the labouring convicts. The financial division was into classes indicating those with and those without allowances with numerous sub-divisions all according to scale of allowance thus :

Male Convicts	**Female convicts**
1. Supervison	Supervision
(a) Jamadar	(a) Jamadar
(b) Tindal	(b) Tindal
(c) Peon	(c) Peon
Labouring Convicts	**Labouring convicts**
(d) 3rd Class	(d) 1st class A
(e) Chain gang	(e) 1st class B
(f) Domestic servants	(f) 2nd class
(g) Self-supporters	(g) Refractory ward
(h) Hospital servants	(h) Self-supporters

Discipline

There were also discipline gangs all involving degradation either on account of bad character on arrival or while in the settlement. They were known as Cellular Jail prisoners, Viper Islands Disciplinary, Chatham Disciplinary, Chain gang, habitual criminal gang, unnatural crime gang and ticket them. During the early part of the twentieth century the penal system had been extended considerably due to demand from the many quarters including the provincial government of India. The then chief commissioner R.C. Temple gave a statement before the Andaman Committee. Though his statement was lauded the British approach without mentioning the atrocities, all the same it gives the legal structure of the penal settlement. The statement runs as follows:

> ".... The convict comes to Andamans a creature, who by his life or his acts, has shown himself to be so unfitting for human society that he has been cast out for life, or for a long terms of years. Received thus, he is first subjected for six months to a most severe discipline - hard, rigid and uncompromising. He is taught it is like to be forced to bend his\uncontrolled nature to the iron yoke of regime, not of hard toil, but of soul crushing monotony. From the stern Cellular Jail he is next transferred to one of the associated jails, to the comparative blessing of hard labour, in company with others but still under strict discipline. He works and feeds with others in gangs, but he still sleeps in his separate cell. Here he stays for a year and half and then for the next three years he is a slave, as the word is ordinarily understood; locked up with other prisoners at night but working in the open at any kind of task that the needs of the settlement may require of him according to his capacity – an unpaid, unrewarded labourers, well-fed, housed, clothed and cared for but always under watch and guard. During the following five years he is still a labouring convict but severity of his life is eased down a little. He is now eligible for the petty post of supervision and for the less irksome and less slave like forms of labour, and he gets very little allowance to buy a few small luxuries, or to place

> in the savings banks for future necessities. Having thus served then long probationary years he is eligible for ticket and becomes what is locally knows as self-supporters. The convict is now in a sense free. He earns his living in his own chosen way, he keeps cattle, he can move about unwatched, he can send for his wife and children, or course he can marry a convict woman, who under her own regulations is eligible for marriage. He can thus become pater familia's with a little hoard of his own earning and differing outwardly in no way from the ordinary villager. In reality, however, he differs greatly that he misses all those things that 'free' men prize so highly. He has no civil rights under the ordinary law, and the executive authority deals with all the affairs of his life. He must live where he is told, and generally conduct his life as he is told, he may move about beyond his village and his field by permission only, he cannot leave the settlement, he may not be idle, under pain of a forced return to convict labour. In this state, he remains for ten or fifteen years, according to the crimes that have sent him here, until the happy days come when the order for absolute release is placed in his hands and he goes free as other men"[5].

Indeed women too are treated on the same lines as male convicts but with some gentleness. Further R.C. Temple made a statement in regard to women convicts who are under different charges imposed by the authority concerned and sent to Port Blair penal settlement to bring necessary discipline and correctional reformation. The following statement reveals the plight of women convicts were as follows:

> "the women are dealt with on the same lines, but more gently, as becomes of the gentler sex. For the first three years the convict woman works in the Female jail as a mere slave, fed, house, clothed and card for. Then for two years she is treated to the same easing down of severity as is granted to the men, and after a total of

five years she is eligible for marriage and domestic service. Assuming that she marries, she joins her husband in the village where she leads the ordinarily life of an Indian women, but subjected to the same disabilities, as her husband until she has completed fifteen years in transportation when she may go free with him whither so ever he may go".[6]

Self-Supporter Status

There is a sharply marked division of the settlement into what was known as the "free" and "convict" portions by which the free settlers living in villages are separated from the ticket-of-leave (self-supporters) convicts also living in the villages. Every effort is made to prevent unauthorized communication between these two divisions. No adult person can enter the settlement without permission or reside without an annual license, and certain other necessary restrictions are imposed on him as to his movements among and his dealings with the convicts etc, the three sub-divisions are Ross Island, Haddo, the convicts sub-division is Viper and Wimberlaygung and the Jail sub-division. The population of the settlement at Port Blair was distributed over the cleared area surrounding the harbour of its name. The extent of the country included within the area was roughly 330 sq.miles and consists of arable land and pasture, interspersed with patches of forest land.

For administrative purpose a line is running roughly north and south into two districts, the Eastern and the Western, divides the settlement. Three districts are further sub-divided into sub-divisions, the headquarters station of the settlement is on a small island called Ross Island in the mouth of the harbour and here are concentrated the principal government officers and the garrison of the settlement. The remaining of the official population is to be found at the district headquarters at Aberdeen and Viper Island or at the several sub-divisions headquarters. The police have their headquarters at Aberdeen, but occupy station and posts throughout the settlement for the maintenance of law and order and for the prosecution of their ordinary police duties. The convict population may be generally divided into three heads:

- Those incarcerated in the jails at Aberdeen and South Point;
- The labouring convicts who were distributed in stations throughout both the districts of the settlement, where they are accommodated in barracks, and were employed on the mechanical and manual labour necessary for the maintenance and development of the settlement; and
- The self-supporters who by service of atleast 10 years with good record consistent as labouring convicts, have earned the privilege of ticket-of-leave. These are located principally in villages on the western district, where they cultivate land, or earn a livelihood by working at the craft of their caste, or at any other they may have earned during their period as labouring convicts.
- Lastly there is an ever increasing free population consisting principally of ex-convicts and their offspring to the third and fourth generation. They are to be found on the eastern districts, where they occupy villages, cultivate land, or carry on business or and craft in the same way as the self-supporters convicts on the western district.[7]

The first step towards the domestication of the convict was his acquisition of self-supported status. The dual purpose behind granting the self-support system to relieving the government of its maintenance cost and making the settlement self-sustaining. Self-supporters were first class prisoners who had been granted a ticket-of-leave and allowed to take up any profession of their choice for a living. In the beginning they were supported by the settlement, but once settled into the new occupation, they had to pay taxes and cesses. These convicts lived in villages around the settlement, cultivated land, kept cattle, became shopkeepers, dhobis, shoe-makers, tailors or barbers or entered into domestic or government service as clerk, compounders, *daftries* or *munshis*. The one engaged in agriculture or manufacturing sold their products to the Commissariat Department and also to other convicts. While these privileges and indulgences made the life of a self-supporter infinitely comfortable and hardly gave civil freedoms and rights to these convicts. There was also a condition that the self-supporter unable to generate enough money and failed to sustain himself after the initial grace period was denounced to a lower grade. The convict had to earn the privilege of becoming a self-supporter and continue exerting himself thereafter to remain solvent, lest he be degraded. The system did not pay immediate financial and economic dividends to the state but was nevertheless upheld right to the twentieth century.

However all the convicts to arrive on the Andamans were male and were lone individuals without kin, family and friends. Indeed this was one of the major hurdles in settling the convicts. The penal authorities tried to emigrate families of ex-convict to prevent the social and unnatural vice; and second it was seen as helping in raising an indigenous population for the purpose of colonization. 'the impossibility of building up a home and family deters many male convicts from settling in Andamans who would, if they get their wives, contentedly stay there and add to the productive powers of the colony.... Convicts with families would be the only men with real interest in the colony'.[8]

Thus, the importation of convict families was seen as the best mode of ensuring the stability of convict households and providing permanency to the labour arrangements. The inducement offered to the families of the convicts for emigration was primarily the permission to reclaim and cultivate land free of rent during their own and their wife's life time. They were also to be given assistance during the first three years by the settlement administration.[9] In the initial years of the settlement's existence the question of family emigration was treated practically as if the settlement was rather a colony of emigrants, than a penal settlement and so long as the political convicts were detained in the Cellular Jail. The first batch of convicts irrespective of their sentence, crime, or conduct on the settlement was asked to send for their families. For the purpose, two Convict Family Emigration Agents were recruited. They were Lalla Mundan Singh for Bengal and Lalla Ram Dayal for the North-west Province and Oudh, each on a salary of Rupees fifty, with a bonus of Rupees two for each female and juvenile member of a family dispatched from Calcutta. They were both put under the orders of the Cooly Emigration Agent in Calcutta.[10] However in short time the government realized that in order to maintain discipline in the colony, the importation of families and the grant of land could not remain an absolute or unreserved right. It was to be a boon that was granted by the administration as a reward to the convict for his good behaviour, hard work and diligence.[11] The convicts on their part were not totally convinced about the government's intentions, most desisted from sending for their families because they feared for their well-being but some nevertheless agreed to apply.[12] There were nearly two hundred convicts who were willing to take a chance and made such applications. In order to encourage the scheme, the government went as far as to give sanctions to the servants and family members of the convicts to be shipped to the Andamans for a preliminary visit. But the response of the families of the convicts was not very encouraging. Most of them sent back negative replies. Out of the 266 letters dispatched there were only twelve cases in which females acquiesced to join their convict relations. Most of the families rejected the offer on account of caste taboos, as Hindu families hesitated to embark on a British vessel fearing loss of caste. By 1860, the settlement officers acknowledged that all efforts to induce the families of the convicts to join them at the Andamans have entirely failed. The idea of convict family migration was never absolutely abandoned and was taken up once again in 1864 by the then superintendent Major Ford. He saw the convict family emigration scheme was 'very expedient and quite practicable' and felt that it would be the first step to colonization'.[13] The only objection he observed would be on grounds of increased expenses. In spite of sincere efforts by various superintendents, the convict family emigration scheme never really paid the expected dividends and very few families actually joined the convicts in the Andamans.

Administration

The penal settlement was administered by the Chief Commissioner of Andaman and Nicobar islands as a superintendent with a deputy and staff of assistant superintendent and oversees. Almost all were Europeans and warder who are natives of India. All the petty supervising establishments themselves were convicts. There were besides these special departments like police, medical, commissariat, forest, tea, marine, and so on. Of the usual type in India except that all civil officers are invested with special powers over convicts. Civil and criminal justice was administered by the series of courts under the Chief Commissioner and deputy superintendent as the principal courts of original and appellate jurisdiction. The chief commissioner was also the chief revenue and financial authority.

Revenue System

All the land in the penal settlement is vested in the crown and all rights in it are subjected to the orders of the government of India. Practically the land was held at a fixed rent under license from the chief commissioner on conditions, which inter alia, subject devolution and transfer to his consent and determine the occupation on completion at a years notice or on breach of the conditions. The working rule framed primarily to meet the requirements of the self-supported convicts was in the hands of the district officers, through alternative revenue officials. Village revenue papers like those maintain in India are kept and fixed survey fees are demanded.[14]

Civil Conditions

The civil conditions in the settlement were not up to the mark and as being of interest was the very small portion of childhood marriages. These were no doubt partly due to the fact that among the children of convict parents government does not recognize marriages where the respective ages of the boys and girl was less than 12 and 10 years. This fact has no doubt a certain influence on the custom throughout the settlement, even among the free and ex-convicts settlers, who are of course placed under no such restrictions. Owing to the paucity of women, polygamy was almost unknown, and as noted elsewhere the breaking down of the caste system, coupled with the absence of public opinion as a check on the actions of individuals has resulted in the most chaotic conditions with regard to marriage among the free population in the settlement. The number of female convicts who were available for marriage was however very less and the proportion of men to women in a convict village was 10 or sometimes 20 to 1.[15] The populations consist of principally adults, and where there were only a small locally born population. Of the population of Port Blair rather more than 70 per cent are convicts for whom no educational facilities were provided. It is the proportion of literates in this large majority which is the principal factor in determining the proportion in the population as a whole. The degree of literacy among the convicts as a whole is probably higher than among the new arrivals alone, as literate convicts are in general demand by the officers of the settlement for employment as writers and *munshis* or as godown keepers or in the other posts where knowledge of reading and writing were essential. Vernacular schools are provided by government throughout the settlement, in some of which introduction in English was also given. The attendance as at these schools was compulsory in the case of the children of convicts between certain ages; moreover education in the settlement was so cheap and its advantages are so well understood that a large proportion of the free and ex-convicts settlers avail themselves of the facilities offered and send their children to school.

The circumstances affecting the composition of the population of the penal settlement are so entirely different from those found elsewhere in India. Later in the middle of twentieth century the community developed into a healthy community in India. Every religion in India was represented among the convicts, but it was impossible to segregate due to mix up. Due to limited interaction and intermixing the people of these islands developed a distinct culture above to all narrow mindedness and chaunistic feelings. It has completely eliminated caste from its social system and religion was very personal. Indeed the social set-up was completely free from any prejudice. Indeed the penal settlement in Andamans has all the administrative appendages including military, post office, electricity and full-fledged system to maintain a colony or settlement. The penal system was primarily one the discipline consideration giving way to the important point. The convict was firstly disciplinary, secondly, it provides for wants of the settlement so far as these can be supplied locally and thirdly, it is for establishment of colony and maintained for strategic importance.

The geographical factors greatly influenced the pattern of penal system in Andamans. Broadly speaking the penal system in Andamans was concerned with crime and its punishment in colonial India. There were serious problems with the manner in which the colonial state punished the male and female offenders and few cases highlighted the quality of the system being implemented in remotest part of the India. The penal authorities were under the impression that the voice of these prisoners would not travel beyond the islands. But much of their annoyance the convict prisoners were successfully managed to dispatch secretly the news about subhuman living conditions, the tale of sufferings and torture. The penal system in Andamans repressive, humiliated, insubordination, homosexuality and general despondency among the convicts because of lack of personal and social ties and rightly termed that Andamans as a 'hellish inferno', the land of death. It also recounts the untold story of the Andamans penal order, where the convicts experienced 'social death', the 'Kalapaani' known for brutality, violence and repression which have been associated with the history of the Andamans.[16]

The basic objective of the penal order in Andamans was to teach the untaught, the stubborn and the defiant. To penetrate, indeed the penal authorities have used all such actions, which were termed inhuman and intolerable. Like any prison, the convicts were forced to do hard work and sometimes the authorities go beyond the purely punitive, the work that long-term convicts performed served certain ideological imperatives. In the context of a criminality it defined substantially in terms of idleness, prison labour and vocational education. It trained men and women in the moral value of work that was stable and visible, and that was properly subordinated to the authority of the British, the authority of men.

The early convicts were all sent to Andaman Island, but by the 1900s they were also being sent directly to destinations such as Viper Island, Nancowre Island, and North Bay. Twenty per cent of these first convicts were women. The majority of women prisoners, and many free women seeking employment, were sent to the 'female factories' as unassigned women. British founded a system of labour in which people, whatever their crime, were employed according to their skills - as brick makers, carpenters, servants, cattlemen and farmers. Educated prisoners were set to the relatively easy work of record-keeping for the convict administration. Women prisoners were assumed to be most useful as wives and mothers, and marriage effectively freed a woman convict from her servitude. From 1858, convicts were seen as a source of labour to advance and develop the British colony. Convict labour was used to develop the public facilities of the colonies-roads, causeways, bridges, courthouses and hospitals. Convicts also worked for free settlers and small land holders. The discipline of labour was seen to be the best chance of reform. The assignment of convicts to private employers was expanded in the 1860s and 1870s, the period when most convicts were sent to the colonies, and this became the major form of employment. Convicts formed the majority of the colony's population for the first few decades, and by 1861 there was a growing number of freed convicts who were appointed to positions of trust and responsibility as well as being granted land.

Good Behaviour and 'Ticket of Leave' Licences

Good behaviour meant that convicts rarely served their full term and could qualify for a Ticket of Leave, Certificate of Freedom, Conditional Pardon or even an Absolute Pardon. This allowed convicts to earn their own living and live independently. However, for the period of their sentence they were still subject to surveillance and the ticket could be withdrawn for misbehaviour. This sanction was found to work better in securing good behaviour than the threat of flogging. The ticket of leave licences were developed first to save money, but they then became a central part of the convict system which provided the model for later systems of probation for prisoners. Firstly, tickets of leave were issued to any convict who seemed able to support himself, and in order to save on providing them with food from the government stores. The tickets were then used as a reward for good behaviour and special service, such as informing on bushrangers. Gentlemen convicts were issued with tickets on their arrival in the colony although finally the British set down regulations for eligibility. Convicts normally sentenced to seven year terms could qualify for a Ticket of Leave after four years, while those serving 14 years could expect to serve between six to eight years. 'Lifers' could qualify for their 'Ticket' after about 10 or 12 years. Those who failed to qualify for a pardon were entitled to a Certificate of Freedom on the completion of their term.

Construction of Cellular Jail

The proposal for the construction of Cellular Jail was devised in 1890 on the recommendations of the Lyall and Lethbridge committee, but it was completed only in 1906. Before the Cellular Jail was constructed, prisoners used to be housed in barracks in Port Blair, the Ross Island and also in concrete structures on Viper Island. The Lyall and Lethbridge Committee consisting of C.J. Lyall of Bengal Civil Service and Surgeon Major A.S. Lethbridge, inspector-general of jails, Bengal inspected the penal settlement at Port Blair in January 1890. Members of this committee reached the Andamans by S.S. Peshwa on 20th January 1890. They stayed there for approximately two weeks and left Port Blair by the same ship on 7th February 1890. The detailed report was submitted by them to the British government on 26th April 1890, a copy of which is available in National Archives, (Home, Port Blair 1890 No. 74 to 78). Colonel Cadell was the jail superintendent during that time. Among other things, the committee suggested in their report to increase the harshness of confinement in the Andamans by keeping the convicts confined in the cells of a restricted area. The doctrine, followed was that a "prison regime must be punitive and humiliating even more dreadful than hangman's noose" so as to employ deterrence through fear both against those subjected to it and for the 'potential dangers' in general. With this objective, the proposal of the committee to construct the Cellular Jail was approved by the government. Originally, the Andaman and Nicobar Manual Settlement Order No. 423 dated 13th September, 1893 was issued for taking up the work of constructing the Cellular Jail right away, as the completion of the jail was considered to be a matter of great urgency. It was to be completed on priority so as to receive the first batch of convicts in October 1896. The jail was to hold 600 prisoners and was to be built at an estimated cost of Rs. 5,17,352 (cash expenditure Rs. 95,881) with McQullen, sub-engineer serving as in-charge of the construction work. But the actual construction of the Cellular Jail was taken up in October 1896.

To speed up the construction work, human resource convicts from different stations like Viper, Navy Bay, Phoenix Bay, Brichgunj, Dundas point etc., were dictated to work in the jail building. At the same time, the southern divisional officer was directed to arrange 20, 000 cubic feet of stone broken up every month by the Viper inmates there. Apart from locally available material, building material was also brought here in enormous quantities from Burma. Sir Richard Temple was the Chief commissioner of Andamans. By 1897 although around 400 cells of the Cellular Jail were ready for occupancy, yet it could be completed only in 1906. It was built on the seacoast at Atlanta Point in Aberdeen at a height of 60 feet from the sea level. The Cellular Jail was a 'pucca' brick structure giving the appearance of a massive fortress. Almost all the political prisoners who have written their memoirs have made reference to the structure, its location and the inner details of the jail. Bejoy Kumar Sinha compared it to the "England's manorial castles that had imprisoned many who were for the march of history against the decaying, parasitic feudalism".

End of Transportation

The last shipment of convicts disembarked in Andaman Island in 1932, the total number of transported convicts stood at around, 40,000 men and women. They were transported to Andaman islands on approximatley 806 ships. The transportation of convicts to Andaman Island ended at a time when the colonies' population stood at around fifty thousand, compared to less than 20, 000 in 1921. By the mid-

1900s there were enough people here to take on the work, and enough people who needed the work. The colonies could therefore sustain themselves and continue to grow. The convicts settlement had served their purpose. While the vast majority of the convicts to Andaman Islands were eastern and northern India (70%), South Indians (24%) remaining Anglo-Indian including (5%), the convict population had a multicultural flavour. Some convicts had been sent from various British outposts such as India and North-west frontiers. There were also Karens from Burma, and non-convict Indian origin population to meet forest requirments and other allied activites. A large number of soldiers were transported for crimes such as mutiny, desertion and insubordination. Most of the Bhantus were thieves who had been convicted in the great cities of united provinces. Only those sentenced in united provinces were likely to have been convicted of rural crimes. Transportation was an integral part of the English system of punishment. It was a way to deal with increased poverty and the severity of the sentences for larceny. Simple larceny, or robbery, could mean transportation for seven years. Compound larceny - stealing goods worth more than a shilling (about $50 in today's money) - meant death by hanging. Men had usually been before the courts a few times before being transported, whereas women were more likely to be transported for a first offence. The great majority of convicts were working men and women with a range of skills.

The Abolition of Transportation

Transportation to the colony of Andaman Islands was officially abolished on 1939, and in 1945 the order to abolish transportation to Andaman Island was formally announced.

The decline of penal colony of Andaman Island was evident from their very beginning. The penal colony and the policies regarding them were not created to last permanently. In the early phase of the penal colony, mostly former prisoners and unwanted religious minorities were transported to the islands. Penal colony was established to increase the number of population, and to serve this purpose, voluntary immigrants were not enough. However, in the later phase of the penal colony, the number of non-convicts increased drastically. Therefore, as the policy achieved its goals, the need for immigrants subsided. This meant that additional labour in a form of indentured servants or forced prisoners could now be replaced with labour of legal or non-convict immigrants. Furthermore, religious minorities were no longer forced to live on the penal colonies because the mercantilist European governments deemed them important to gaining more wealth of the nation. Moreover, from the political point of view, as the civil rights increased, such inhumane practice of removing people from their homeland was deemed illegal. For example, although France kept transporting criminals to the notorious Devil's Island even until late as early 20th century, the government lost its ground for holding the penal colony when the imprisonment of Alfred Dreyfus who was wrongfully sent there revealed the notorious treatment and inhumane practices in the penal colony. Public outcry started to gather against such outdated practices and eventually led to the end of penal colonies in France. These two reasons cooperated with each other to stop the practice of penal sentence altogether. In 1938 the French government stopped sending prisoners to Devil's Island, and in 1952 the prison closed forever.

Penal colonies came into being because of two reasons. One was political, which enabled the government to simply transport those who cause trouble for the regime, and another was economical, which forced penal labour to turn the colonies into profitable source of wealth quickly. However, pursuing only these two reasons was very costly, because concerns over civil rights and individual basic rights were often ignored. Thousands of people had to suffer far from their homeland, sometimes for just doing minor crimes. The laws were unfavourable toward the poor, and such people easily became victim of penal labour. Of course, developing the frontiers must have been very crucial part of their political achievement for most of the European nations with colonies. However, they accomplished such feat by sacrifice of much human suffering. Some might try to think that attaining the goal of establishing colonies was a task worthy enough for such sacrifices. Yet, none of the sacrifices was voluntary, and involuntary sacrifices are never noble.

The Prison and Colonial Rule in Andaman Islands

The prison system in Andaman Island was a dumping ground. This was evident from the records of Indian Jails Committee Report of 1919-1920. Initially it was presumed that the prisons in Andaman focus more on the correctional reforms of convicted criminals, instilling in him discipline and the habit of hard work. To assert that criminality was not an immutable state was to acknowledge the prospect that crime could be reduced, the criminal might be reformed, the vagrant can be fed, the addict broken and the dacoit disciplined. This was partially true, but the fact remains was that British largely failed to secure its objective 'taught to unteach'. They have established special jails and goals for men aged between 19 and 25, with a demanding labour regime and separate juvenile homes and female jails had been constructed to minimize adulteration and sexual abuse. But all these were piecemeal arrangements and sex related crimes overcast the settlement, became unsafe for children and female to great extent. The overcrowded prisoners were employed through their sentences in labour gangs, making roads or working in government stone quarries to fulfill the settlement civil requirements. The murderers and dacoits were placed along with the political detainees and few of them appointed as warders of convict stations. The provincial administration failed to separate the criminals from freedom fighters. The prison had become more a battle ground than correctional system. It was utter failure to deploy disciplinary practices on the inmates of jail because of the extremely tight-fisted character of the colonial state and its stubborn refusal to provide the resources necessary for the creation of a truly disciplinary panel system. Keeping in view the adverse conditions, the convict transportation was abolished in 1921 with the intention to improve the conditions of the settlement.

But by the 1930s there was a fresh batch of revolutionaries involved in the fierce struggle between the British rule. These political prisoners, returned cellular jail to centre stage. Infact, the prison in Andaman was a political battle ground. This surely reflected the fact that there was sustained hunger strikes. These posed challenge to colonial regime in Andaman. The prison authorities in Andaman have not paid considerable attention to the physical health of the inmates, which caused large number of deaths while in sentence. The poor conditions of living, lack of proper nutritional foods, mental agony and desperation, unhealthy social affairs together deteriorated the health conditions of inmates. A Cellular jail reflects the political imperatives of British regime. The prison system in Andaman was defined in large part by the fact that the prison there became a major coercive mechanism to suppress the voice of political prisoners' independence and self-determination. All kinds of inhuman methods were executed on political prisoners to suppress their voice. The imprisonment of some revolutionary political prisoners brought out the inhuman face of British authority in Andaman jail. The prison thus had a central role in fostering political consciousness among the inmates.

REFERENCES

1. Aparna Vaidik, Settling the convicts : Matrimony and Domesticity in the Andaman, *Studies in History*, Vol. XXII, No-2, New Delhi, July-December 2006. p. 221.
2. *Local Gazetter* 1908, Andaman and Nicobar Islands, Superintendent Press, Calcutta, Government of India, 1908. pp. 90-92.
3. *Ibid.*, pp. 93-94
4. *Ibid.*, p. 94.

5. Tamta. B.R., *Andaman and Nicobar Islands*, National Book Trust of India, New Delhi, 1992. pp. 25-26.
6. *Ibid.*, pp. 26-27.
7. *Ibid.*, pp. 95-96.
8. Home Department, Judicial Proceedings, May 7, 1858, National Archives of India, New Delhi. pp. 24-26.
9. Home Department, Judicial Proceedings, May 7, 1858, National Archives of India, New Delhi. pp. 24-26-NAI.
10. Home Department, Judicial Proceedings, September 24, 1858, pp. 7-9 NAI and Home Department, Judicial Proceedings, Port Blair Bench, May 7, 1858, National Archives of India, New Delhi. pp. 24-26 NAI.
11. Home Department, Judicial Proceedings, Port Blair Bench, July 29, 1859, National Archives of India, New Delhi. pp. 55-58.
12. Home Department, Judicial Proceedings, Port Blair Bench, July 29 1859. NAI, New Delhi. pp. 55-58.
13. Home Department, Judicial, Port Blair Bench, November 18, 1864, NAI, New Delhi. pp. 14-18.
14. Mathur. L.P., *Kala Pani*, Eastern Book Corporation, Delhi, 1985. p. 112.
15. Aparna Vaidik, *op. cit.*, pp. 221-226.
16. *Ibid.*, p. 223.

3
The Saga of Freedom Struggle in Andaman Islands

Historians often claimed that the plan for a penal colony in Andaman Island was under consideration prior to 1857 revolt. However, on verification of evidence from records in this regard reveals that the Andaman penal colony was established only for the culling intellectual class, who actively participated in the 1857 revolt or either contributed literally or mentally. Testifying the fact, Mout in his book "*The Andaman Islands*" mentioned the personal interest taken by Lord Canning, the then Governor-General, who has requested the commission under the chairmanship of Mout to look into the feasibility of establishing a penal settlement at the earliest for the deportation of revolutionaries. This was in spite of the Indian Law Commission which did not favour the transportation of political prisoners. However the Government of India in 1858 decided to deport, in the first instance, prisoners sentenced on charges of mutiny, rebellion and form other offences connected therewith. However, there was growing perception within British intellegencia that the manner in which the colonial state punished the intellectual class in Andaman's opposed all sorts of barbaric punishment inflicted on revolutionaries, but the British media have unsuccessfully tried to cover up this misdeed.

Andaman Islands were closely connected with the saga of Indian struggle for freedom in the remotest part of India. The last decade of nineteenth century and the rise of extremism in Indian politics gave birth to revolutionary as well as militancy movements. During the Swadeshi movement several secret associations and societies were active in Bengal and elsewhere. As a result of the repressive policies of the British government led to various crimes in different provinces of India. The entire political movement was meant for independence and self-rule. Broadly speaking there was a growing perception that there were serious problems with the manner in which the colonial state punished the political prisoners in Andaman Islands. While some observers questioned whether imprisonment in colonial jails was particularly punishing, others expressed alarm that such incarceration was actually counterproductive and that instead of reforming the political prisoners, British contributed to their further demoralization. Keeping in view and to curtail further political agitation, the British chose the Andaman Islands as the best site for political detention. It is generally believed that many political rebels from different parts of the county were deported to Andaman Islands from the ports like Calcutta, Karachi and Madras. In subsequent years more political freedom fighters and other mutineers were transported to these islands. The entire history of transportation of political prisoners has been divided into three major groups and phases:

- First Phase 1858- 1905
- Second Phase 1905-1921
- Third Phase 1932-1938.

First Phase - Heroes of 1858

The Great War sparked on May 1857, fanned by the blood and sacrifices of the martyrs took the form of gigantic fire that engulfed the entire nation. Indeed the first war of independence shocked the British authorities. After the initial setback in putting down the revolution the British were able to tighten their grip. As soon as they recovered from the shock they started devising unconstitutional methods for dealing with the revolutionaries in order to have permanent and effective hold over the country. Hence the search for suitable place for keeping the mutineers became of paramount importance. Meanwhile the Andaman Islands were considered for penal deportation and the job assigned to Captain Mann, who was actually hoisted British flag on 22nd January 1858 along with a team of officials.

The Hero's of 1857 war of Independence were mostly revolutionary freedom fighters. They belonged to rich and well to do micro section of Indian society- zamindars, Nawabs, writers, poets and soldiers, who fought bravely for the cause of motherland. This great revolution which began as a mere spark in May 1857, fanned by the blood and sacrifice of the martyrs, took the form of a gigantic fire which engulfed the entire nation. To crush the movement the British authorities had taken all methods with iron hand and no body let free who have participated in the revolt against the state. One such measure was sending the revolutionaries to Andaman Islands with a hidden intention to execute stringent punishment and by segregating and separating the mutineers by which the freedom movement can be crushed in no time.

Dr. James Petition Walker along with 500 political mutineers sailed out from Calcutta for Port Blair on 4th March 1858. The voyage was not so smooth. Setting sail from Calcutta, often in deplorable conditions, the journey took anywhere between a week and several didn't make it to their final destination and finally the ship reached Port Blair on 10th March 1858.[1] In subsequent years more prisoners were sent in different batches. With this the Indian nationalism marked the beginning in far away territory from mainland India. The political detainees have seen the worst side of imperialism and colonialism confronted with adverse losses humanily face. Most mutineers were met with untold miseries and sufferings. The British officers-in-charge of the political convicts tried all sorts of barbaric and savage methods of punishment including summary mass execution. However it is known from the writings of Ghalib, a famous Urdu poet, that his friend Allami Fazil Haq 'Khairabadi', was transported to the 'Kala paani. Khairabadi died in Andaman during the period of sentence. Maulana Liaquat Ali, from Kanpur, another famous leader of the mutineers also breathed last in Kala Paani. Other prominent leaders including Ramnauth (Lucknow), Shewdeen (Pratapgarh), Mohammud Bux (Lucknow), Koonj Baharee (Lucknow), Ahbar Ali (Lucknow), Khoda Bux (Lucknow), Koor Singh (Ludhiana), Mohammed Jan (Peshawar), Hurdeo Singh (Kanpur), Juggur Nath (Poorwah), Panchum Singh (Guddree kheriah) and other great sons of the motherland were brutally punished and inflicted the great horror of being exiled. From Assam, Dante Ram Barman, Sheikh Formud Ali, Madhu Malik and Bahadurgoan Burah were also transported to Kala Paani. The punishment was intolerable and perpetual victimhood and lost all face of humanity. One such example was Raja Loni Singh of Mitauli, who extended hand to Oudh king. Loni Singh appealed against the trial and judgment to Her Majesty – Queen of England. But the aged and ailing Raja obtained neither remission nor redressed to his grievances. His appeal was rejected in November 1859 and pressed an order for deportation to Port Blair. On his way to the Kala Pani, the Raja died 'as a result of refusal to take food'.

The back-breaking, hard manual labour they were subjected to under semi- starved conditions amounted to sub-human living and resulted in innumerable deaths. The officials were fully aware that they were 'men who have been led to the commission of crimes against the state by the example of others and not men of a desperate or unmanageable character'. The official communiqué also described them as not the people who belonged to the lower strata of society either they were all sepoys, zamindars and maulavis – people who were politically conscious, knowledgeable, comparatively well of who loved their country and fought for it. The life of torture, intimidation, misery and humiliation did not kill the entire spirit in them was evident from the fact that there were charges of conspiracy, of inciting to rebel etc., against many political detainees. Nearly all of them perished under agonizing circumstances. The patriots of 1857 died unhonoured, unlamented and unsung in the remotest part, but they will be remembered for their valiant spirit and profound determination to make the most out of unambiguously rough circumstances.

The plight of mutineers who were transported to Kala paani on charges of waging war against the British empire 1857 were treated at par with other criminals for seditious crimes. The unbearable and inhuman treatment led to fleeing of many prisoners from the custody. Few of them died due to extremity and starvation; few might have been killed by aboriginals and eighty-six prisoners who were recaptured were hanged by the colonial government to prevent future escapes; and to create a fear in the minds of other prisoners. One such incident draws attention of the cruelty of the regime. One sepoy mutineer Shri. Narain,[2] was shot by Walker, then the superintendent of settlement, was trying to escape from a boat by swimming across the channel.

Political prisoner experiences

The ship 'Semirami' sailed from Calcutta to Port Blair, the first batch of rebels had witnessed a horrendous journey, and the day when they embarked the ship they were confronted with all such the inhuman atrocities. The journey took approximately 5 large days and seemed approaching unknown destiny, nothing was visible except blue water and sky - at a distance it looked like that was the end, where the sky touched the sea. As belief goes in those days beyond the limit of sky and earth, there was hell. Infact the Andaman Islands were no less then hell and beyond hell and horrific as mentioned by the prisoners who were deported to the islands. After few days, the blue waters gradually changed colour to black and the day became smaller and shorter. Finally they sighted a small island floating in splendid isolation in the middle of the sea, which was horrifying for onlookers who hadn't experienced ever before. Hardly anybody heard the sweet tunes of a cuckoo or even sighted single bird except flying fish during the voyage. Finally on the 7th day the ship anchored and allowed the political prisoners to disembark on a land where they failed to get portable water under heavy summer. Due to heavy humidity the prisoners felt uneasiness and to few of them hostile conditions were unbearable by nature and authority. Nobody dare to imagine the hard conditions which prevailed on the islands. Especially, the political prisoners were subjected to soul crushing labour under hostile conditions and were whipped mercilessly for the slightest lapse. The arrangements for food, cloth and shelter were not adequate; they were under semi-starvation and lived under the open sky for several days. They were subject to all kinds of natural hazards and they often left to fend for themselves, without any kind of protection in places where a single arrow from the aboriginals was enough to kill them. The idea of giving the arms for self- defence against aboriginals was not even considered because J.P. Walker had warned of any leniency in this regard. In his letter dated May 7th 1858, Secretary, Government of India in the Home Department writes to Walker....

> "... The President in Council desired me particularly to caution you against being lulled into a false sense of security by the absence of any apparent intent or desire on the part of the convicts to defy our authority. The firearms of the guard should be always loaded and it should be impossible, to get them into their hands for a moment, and the guard should always be ready to fire at once on the shortest notice".

The untold sorrows, miseries and sufferings compelled them to prefer death and few of them self-hanged because of unbearable tortures inflicted. It will be difficult to erase the memories of the shameful acts of cruelty and barbarism let loose towards revolutionary freedom fighters by the British. One such incident was quoted by an Urdu intellegentia, who had been transported to Andaman Islands on mere involvement by expressing his view through writing. The Fadl-e-Haqq mentioned the pathetic condition of imprisonment in his genre of prisoner poetry (Habsiyyat) narrates his experience of deportation to the Andaman Islands.

> "... the hardhearted enemies then brought him to an island i.e., the Andamans, where the sun would constantly shine right on his head and where difficult hilly paths and dangerous roads made walking impossible. The air was extremely warm and amenities more bitter than poison. The sky resembled one big looming cloud, which kept pouring out nothing but sorrows. The earth looked dotted with measles and pocks, and from the roofs of the houses there were only drops falling like the tears from his eyes. The air was contaminated and therefore a constant source of ailments. Often there were epidemics. The sick had no chance to be cured; the sane was bereft of security. The one who cured disease became ill, and the one who was sick was definite prey for death. There was no empathy and pity whatsoever, no disease was not fatal. Every disease ultimately led to death, even Hypochondria and Pleurisy. There were diseases totally unknown and very dangerous. The doctor could not come up with a diagnosis; instead he gave medicines which wrecked the patient. If a prisoner dies, an unclean person looking like devil or monster (Shaitan Khannas) would come to drag the corpse away by the feet, take off his clothes and dig the corpse into a sand hill without a coffin and bury it without performing ablution. As there was no grave and no burial, one did not wish to die. If suicide was not illegal all prisoners would have taken recourse to it. It was in such an environment that he fell ill and succumbed to depression. Moreover, he got worms and other diseases and although his body was aching, he was made to walk and exercise in the mornings and evenings. Soon he would die, after a prosperous and

enjoyable life, when he was old and insane, wounded and ulcerated. But still he thanked God for His mercy because next to him he saw sick prisoners in chains, who were brought to their daily working place by a terrible man who did not show any empathy whatsoever. Khairabadi thanked God for having saved him from these atrocities. Having full belief in God, he asked the creator in the name of Prophet Muhammad, to free him from that horrifying situation and fulfill the divine promise to listen to the destitute".

Certainly the political prisoners would have preferred death to such a pathetic existence and were prepared to attempt an escape at the least opportunity, but where could they escape? There was the fathomless expanse of the ocean all around and even on land they were surrounded by hostile aboriginals. M.V. Portman narrates a daring attempt of escape by one prisoner named Narain. "On the fourth day after arrival Convict No. 61, made an attempt to escape from Chatham by swimming to the nearby island and nearly succeeded. However, he was captured by a boat crew convicted for sedition and escape and was executed". Within a few days Narain committed suicide in Ross Island. In another incident on March 18, 1858, 21 freedom fighters escaped in a raft from Ross Islands, similarly on March 23, 1858 another eleven political convicts escaped from Ross headquarters; however they were brutally killed by the aboriginals. According to Walker, "in a debilitated state from want of food and water and covered with vermin, that infested even his ears and eyelids adhering so firmly that he could not remove them. They had been duped by a fellow prisoner who pretended to have held communication with aboriginals who promised help on the part of the Raja. When they left, 100 aboriginals attached and killed the leader".

The tortures inflicted by the authorities were increased day by day. The prisoners were handcuffed together in pairs and these handcuffs were never opened. The acute discomfort and mental agony that the prisoners had to undergo in attending to the calls of nature, eating, bathing and sleeping can well be imagined. They were punished severely for the slightest lapse in their work. During working hours a number of them were taken to the sea beach and an iron bar was passed through the fetters. They were thus fastened to the earth and made to do what work they could do in a sitting position.

The authorities in charge of the political convicts tried all sorts of barbaric and savage methods of punishment including summary mass execution. The back-breaking hard manual labour and semi-starved conditions amounted to sub-human living and resulted in innumerable deaths. When the tortures inflicted upon them became unbearable, the prisoners made desperate plans for escape. In one dead night nearly 100 prisoners escaped from Ross islands by using bamboo poles tied with creepers made rafts and crossed sea and ventured to unknown destinations, embracing roaring waves of the vast ocean. Perhaps they knew their end had come but at least they had the satisfaction of embracing death as free men. It was adventure to think of crossing the high seas on bamboo rafts, since it was a case of sure suicide.

Meanwhile the Governor-General specifically asked Dr. Walker not to extend capital punishment to political convicts on the charges of escaping. However Dr. Walker conceived it was necessary to rule the convicts with a severity which was perhaps carried to the extreme. Awarding death penalty on charges of escaping from legal custody was an inhuman act and not found in any jurisprudence. Ignoring the orders of the Governor- General Dr. Walker sentenced to death all those convicts who attempted to escape, considered that he was acting in the best interest of discipline, but the fear of capital punishment did not deter the political convicts. The health of the mutineers deteriorated day by day due to bad climate, hard labour and absence of proper food making life impossible to survive. In 1863 Robert Napier visited the settlement and found that most of the convicts had tattered clothes and bad state of health conditions. A mere look at the Jail Manual of 1874 shows that it was deliberately kept low by the government, the punishment of transportation was defined as follows:

"Transportation entails hard labour with strict discipline, with only such food as is necessary for health. Any mitigation of the above is an indulgence which may at any time be withdrawn in whole or in part". The Government of India directed Colonel Henry Man, the first superintendent of Penal settlement to place persons, who were led to the commission of crime against the state in the third class only. In the opinion of Raffles, the third class, who were regarded on harder scales of labour and solitary confinement in the night, known as Penang rules. Then the chief commissioner R.C. Temple gave a statement before the Andaman commission. Though the statement lauds the British approach without mentioning the atrocities, all the same it gives the legal structure of the penal settlement. The statement runs as follows: ".... The convict comes to Andaman a creature, who by his life or his acts, has shown himself to be so unfitting for human society that he has been cast out of it for life, or for a long term of years. Received thus, he is first subjected for six months to almost severe discipline-hard, rigid, uncompromising. He is taught what it is like to be forced to bend his uncontrolled nature to the iron yoke of a regime, not of hard toil, but of soul crushing monotony. From the stern jail he is next transferred to one of the associated jails, to the comparative blessing of hard labour, in company with others but still under strict discipline. He works and feeds with others in gangs, but he still sleeps in his separate cell. Here He stays for a year and a half and then for the next three years he is a slave, as the word is ordinarily understood ; locked up with other prisoners at night but working in the open at any kind of task that the needs of the settlement may require of him according to his capacity.

The Wahabi movement was considered one of the most seditious movements of the nineteenth century, and therefore British officers were rather cautious in granting pardon. In 1865, Wahabi prisoners were transported to the Penal system in large number. With the influx of Wahabi prisoners the problems of the islands were on high. Most of the leaders died in the isle of banishment and others suffered the rigorous life of the Kala Pani – 'hellish inferno' the land of death. Mohammand Jafar Thanesari[3] a Wahabi Maulavi from Thanesar in Ambala district, Punjab, who was convicted in 1865 and arrived in the Andamans in 1868. He lived in the Andamans for twenty years and on his return to India wrote a memoir in Urdu called *Kala pani ya Tarikh-i-Ajeeb*. It presents a lively account of his life as a convict in the penal settlement. Jafar Ali has vividly described the murder of Lord Mayo in 1872. According to him the murderer Sher Ali, was a frustrated Wahabi and wanted to overthrow the government. In 1891 some of the followers of Senapati Tikendrajit, who were hanged by the British authorities for leading the revolt in Manipur in 1890, were transported to the Andamans. These prisoners belonging to the royal family were interned in bungalow on Mount Harriet. Thus the political detainees were treated differently from the common criminals. Hard labour in extreme weather conditions, invalid diet and malaria caused most deaths. Meanwhile a large number of Burmese of Tharawada, who revolted against the British, were also transported to Andamans.

Second Phase – Andaman Nationalism

Extremism marked a phase in Bengal politics characterized by political violence by a youthful section of the 'Hindu Badralok' class mainly during the first three decades of the twentieth century. The emergence of revolutionary terrorism coincided with the partition of Bengal (1905) and moderate and extremist rift in the Indian National Congress. Ideologically, the participants in the politics of violence were directly influenced by the radical thoughts of Bankimchandra Chatopadhyay, Swami Vivekananda and Sri Aurobindo Ghosh, in their philosophies and thoughts that the revolutionary ideas and vocabularies of the revolutionaries were rooted. Their thoughts led the youth to seek strength from the distant past in order to oust the colonial rulers from India by force. The participating youths were devoted to the cult of 'shakti' and its associated cult of *Dharmarajya Samsthapan*. They took oath to kill the demons (foreign rulers) and renew the cosmic realm of Hindu civilization based on classical Brahmanical purity.

The revolutionaries were organized into two major groups: Calcutta Jugantar and Dhakha Anuseelan Samity. Their activities were conducted with utmost secrecy. Special codes were adopted to maintain the secrecy of their operations. Those who were initiated as revolutionaries were under vow not to divulge their plans and programmes to anybody, not even to parents. Consequently, many parents never knew that their school or college going sons were, in fact, active members of one or other revolutionary groups. During the Swadeshi movement several secret societies were active in the Bengal and other parts of the country. First, the appalling heartlessness of the most sophisticated nation on earth (England) to crush the Swadeshi Movement; and second, the stirring picture of revolutionaries, taking up the challenge and proceeding to "beat the system" against incalculable odds. It was thought that by sending revolutionaries to the Andaman Islands, it would become more useful to Great Britain for temporary halt in the resistance to consolidate their position in pre-World War I. This practice was continued until the Second World War. A large number of political activists were imprisoned on various charges in different provinces of India were sent Andaman islands to the presumption that they will never return to mainland India. In 1909, Sir John Hewett, the Governor of the United Provinces, proposed the transportation of two seditionists named Ram Hari and Hoti Lal Verma to the Kala Pani. Both of them were the editors of a newspaper named *'Swarajya'* published from Allahabad. Lord Minto, the then Governor General of India refused to transport them to the Andamans, because the Imperial Legislature had already suspended the deportation of term convicts to far away place.

Similar request was made by the Lt. Governor of Bengal in December 1909 to grant necessary permission to transport prisoners sentenced for various terms in the Alipore Bomb Case. These prisoners included Barinder Kumar Ghosh, the brother of Sri. Aurobindo Ghosh, Hem Chandra Das, Ulaskar Datta, Indu Bhusan Roy and others. Keeping in view the inflammable and revolutionary character, the Government of India accorded necessary sanction in March 1910 to transport the political prisoners to Andamans.[4] A large number of political detainees were sent to Andamans from different provinces. They were Hoti Lal Verma, Nand Gopal and Ladha Ram from United Provinces. Eleven prisoners were accused in the Khulna Conspiracy case and Shri. Vinayak Damodar Savarkar, his brother Ganesh Damodhar Savarkar and Wamanji sentenced for various terms in the Nasik Conspiracy case were sent from the Bombay to Kala Pani. It is very difficult to give an exact number of political prisoners sent to Kala Pani in between 1910 to 1920. According to a list published by Ex-political Prisoners Fraternity Circle, Calcutta out of 133 persons who were in the Andamans during this period 81 were from Punjab, 38 from Bengal, 11 from Uttar Pradesh and remaining 3 political prisoners belong to Maharashtra.

The aggressive nationalism had two distinct phases. In the first phase, from 1905 to 1918, the activists were more given up to the restoration of the imagined world of *Dharmarajya* of the *Gita*. During this period, no less than 210 incidents occurred in which 70 police and targeted persons and twenty-four revolutionaries were killed. During the same period, 205 persons were convicted under the Indian Penal Code and Arms and Explosive Substances Acts. A large number of the convicts were transported to the Andaman, the penal settlement of British India off the Bay of Bengal. The First World War situation made the government particularly worried about the revolutionaries. In an effort to contain their activities 1262 persons were detained between 1915 and 1918. Most of them were either cadres of the Anushilan or the Jugantar. As a result of the strong counter measures and vigilance, the revolutionary activities came to a virtual halt by 1919. Only one incident took place in 1919 and none in 1920 and 1921. Satisfied by the improved political conditions and persuaded by the idea of placating the Indian public opinion in favour of constitutional reforms, the government released, under a royal pardon, all political detainees held under the Defence of India Act. The amnesty included the revolutionaries transported to the Andaman as well.

Deportation during 1915-1921 in Cellular Jail

Deportations and capital punishments had increased tremendously during the post World War I period. This was a consequence which led to even more stringent and dishonest measures being taken by the Imperial British, and the Indians boiling up from within to oust these oppressors. The Government of India gave in to the forceful plea of Governor O' Dwyer and under dismal circumstances, the Defence of India Act (1915) was promulgated by which a Special Tribunal for the trial of the persons charged of revolutionary crimes was established. A.A. Irvine was the president and T.R Ellis and R.B. Pandit Sheo Narain were the commissioners. Under this Act, commitment proceedings were dispensed with and the provision of appeal was erased. Many other patriots convicted in fake trials were also sent to the Andaman and Nicobar Islands. Master Chattar Singh Sangla, who under the influence of Ghadr Party attempted to murder Professor Duncliff in the house of the principal of Khalsa College, Amritsar on 16th December 1914 with a *chhawi* (a sharp edged weapon) was arrested. He was prosecuted under Section 307 of the Indian Penal Code and was sentenced to transportation for life. He too, was sent to the Andamans. Sachinder Nath Sanyal was a revolutionary of the first rank. In Benaras, even during his school days, he had formed a club called the 'Anushilan Samiti', which subsequently came to be known as 'Young Men's Association'. In early 1914, Rash Behari Bose virtually took charge of the movement at Benaras with Sachinder as second in command. Sachinder was also a linkage between Punjab Ghadr leaders and Rash Behari Bose. The Bengal revolutionaries also adopted the line of action of Punjab Ghadr leaders and coordinated the armed rebellion in Benaras with armed rebellion finalized by the Punjab Ghadr leaders for 21st February 1915. But the information of the change in date to February 19 could not reach Benaras. Sachinder arrived on 21st February 1915, at the parade ground. He was arrested and booked in Benaras Conspiracy Case which was also heard by the Special Tribunal established under the Defence of India Act. A challan of twenty-five individuals was presented, but sixteen were actually facing the trial. The judgment was announced on 14th February 1916. Sachinder Nath Sanyal was sentenced to expatriation for life, while others were awarded short-term imprisonments. Sachinder Nath Sanyal was sent to the Andaman.

Another patriot sent to the Andaman was Randhir Singh, S/o Natha Singh of Narangwal district Ludhiana. He was a prominent Sikh leader and a literary figure. He led the movement against the British for pulling down a wall of Gurdwara Rakab Ganj in Delhi. He was arrested, prosecuted and sentenced to deportation for life. Govindcharan Kar was another active revolutionary during the First World War period. He was prosecuted and sentenced to seven years rigorous imprisonment and was sent off to the Andamans. After his release, he again participated in the revolutionary activities and was convicted in the Kakori Conspiracy Case. He was sentenced to expatriation for life. The revolutionary patriots in Bengal were also keeping the British administration on tenterhooks by their swashbuckling acts. By the time the police was triggered to nab the people involved in one political crime, another was committed. Some of these astonishing events these brave patriots were involved in and their planning are worth recalling as these patriots were later arrested, tried and sent to the Andaman. The revolutionaries were still fighting for the independence of their country and the government had also let loose the subjugation in full measure. After the Jallianwala Bagh episode, all of India was up in arms against the British. On 15th April 1919, the residents of Chuharkana destroyed the railway bridge, uprooted the railway line and set the railway station on fire. The European police fired back at them. Some were killed, many others were injured and about 400 were arrested. Thirty top leaders, including Teja Singh Chuharkana and Kartar Singh Jabbar were prosecuted. The judgement was announced on 22nd May 1919. Seventeen of them were sentenced to deportation for life, while Kartar Singh Jabbar, Teja Singh Chuharkana, Kahan Singh Chuharkana, Jagir Singh Muridke, Maina Singh Nankherke and Mehar Din Lohar were sentenced to death. On 30th May 1919, however, their death sentences were converted to transportation for life. Teja Singh Chuharkana and Kartar Singh Jabbar were sent to the Andaman. They were released in 1920 as a result of royal compassion. Master Raja Ram of Amritsar was also prosecuted in martial law trials and was sentenced to transportation for life and was sent to the Andaman. Some other patriots convicted and sentenced for political crimes were also sent to the Andaman during 1915-1921, the cases under which they were convicted are yet to be identified.

In the manifesto submitted to the jail authorities the prisoners made three principal demands:

- As political prisoners, they should have all the privileges of the first class;
- That they should, otherwise, be put in the category of ordinary prisoners, given all the facilities allotted

to them and the periodical visit to this jail be permitted to the members of their families; or

- They should be sent back to serve their term in the jails of India, so that they may get all the facilities of that jail life including reduction in the period of the sentence after a certificate of good behaviour.

Obviously the authorities were in no mood to acknowledge any of these demands. They then resorted to another strike in March 1914, the only available weapon with the political prisoners. Almost all of them struck work. Punishments of standing handcuffs, fetters, bar-fetters and reduced diet, one after the other were inflicted on the political prisoners. V.D. Savarkar also joined the strike. Even he was not spared from the rigour of harsh punishments. However, in spite of these punishments, the strike continued. Nani Gopal again resorted to a hunger strike. Savarkar persuaded the hunger strikers to discontinue their strike. They agreed but Nani was unrelenting. His health was getting dangerously affected and was a cause of concern to the other prisoners. When the fellow-prisoners failed to influence him, V.D. Savarkar went on hunger strike to persuade him. It proved successful and Nani resumed eating. Due to this strike, the prisoners were unable to communicate with each other for co-ordinating their activities. The authorities not only lodged them in cells at a distance but guards were also posted to restrict the prisoners from speaking to each other. So the political prisoners hit upon a device to communicate with one another in invented coded language and in signals. The general strike was in full swing. Just about all versions of punishments were exhausted. They were hauled up before the magistrate. Some got two months, some four, while Nani Gopal was given one year's rigorous punishment. But the strike was not withdrawn. Ultimately the Government of India took a final decision on the fate of political prisoners in Andamans in April 1914 and when the orders to that effect reached Andamans in May 1914, the strike resorted to by these prisoners was still going on. The authorities came to terms with the political prisoners and the strike came to an end.

Notification was issued by the authorities to the following effect:

- All the prisoners who were sentenced to a specific period of time, short of life-sentence, shall be sent back to their respective prisons in India, where the reduction of their sentence will be accordingly considered and followed.
- Prisoners for life-sentence shall be detained in the prison for a continuous period of fourteen years, whereafter they will be set free for some labour of light character. This shall operate only in the case of those prisoners who give proof of good behaviour during their period of captivity.
- During the period of fourteen years, the prisoner shall be given decent food to eat, and decent clothes to wear. After five years, he shall be allowed to cook his own food and given from twelve annas to a rupee per month as his pocket allowance.

The following concessions were also offered to the political prisoners:

- The substitution of simple imprisonment in place of rigorous imprisonment as a reward for the good behaviour of the political prisoners;
- light work in place of demanding and degrading type-of work (like grinding of oil);
- supply of books approved by the government;
- grant of occasional holidays (from work);
- grant of same privileges as enjoyed by the ordinary convicts in respect of dress and the writing and receiving letters;
- treatment like ordinary convicts in regard to

punishments deluding whipping; and
- release of life-term political prisoners of good behaviour from the Cellular Jail after 14 years.

Other political prisoners who were to continue their sentence in Port Blair were extended the following facilities:

- The prisoners were allowed in lots to cook their own food.
- Some of them were given work in the printing press, in the library and on map drawing, each earning about Rs. 10 a month from the work. However, V.D. Savarkar and Ganesh Savarkar were not given any of these concessions in the beginning.

The British ultimately could not cripple the fortitude of the revolutionaries, who braved the agonizing situation with great courage. Thus, was started the second phase of revolutionary nationalism. Series of attacks were made on government establishments and persons from 1929 to 1933 including the most sensational Chittagong Armoury raid led by Surya Sen in 1930. Attack was launched even on the governor of Bengal, Sir Stanley Jackson, in February 1932. In 1934 came another gun attack on Governor Sir John Anderson and that was, in fact, the last major revolutionary adventure. The new political development was under the operation of the Act of 1935. The British decision to quit India and the rise of Muslim separatism had completely changed the political edifice on which the revolutionary ideas were built. The Revolutionary Terrorism thus came to an end by 1936.

Cellular Jail: Witness of Sufferings

If there is one place in Andaman Islands which should be visited by every Indian it is Cellualr jail. This magnificently preserved penal identity is a powerful reminder of British's early history. For just a moment forget the beautiful Islands, trees, the neat paths and the green paradise and try to imagine what it must have been like to have lived in the teeming slums of London's East End, to have stolen a bolt of cotton, or some foodstuffs or been involved in some petty crime and, having been sentenced to seven years transportation, to have found yourself at the other end of the world in this god-forsaken institution. The scale of the punishment seems so out of proportion to the crimes which were committed. It is extraordinary to contemplate that 32,500 convicts served their time at Cellular jail between 1906 and 1937. The Cellular Jail was inalienably linked to the long and glorious struggle of our revolutionary freedom movement fought on the mainland and it had deep political significance. Leading figures like Vinayak Damodar Savarkar [5] and his brother Ganesh Damodar Savarkar,[6] Nani Gopal Mukherjee,[7] Bhai Paramanand,[8] Prithvi Singh Azad,[9] Trailakya Maharaj,[10] Ananta Singh and a host of other revolutionary fighters. The list is long and distinguished.

Revolutionaries

The most glaring of them all were the revolutionary freedom fighters from Bengal and other provinces of India during the period from 1909 to 1921. The prominent among these were those from the Mopla rebellion (Kerala) (1892-1927), Second Rumpa Rebellion (Andhra Pradesh) (1922-1924), Tharawadi Peasant rebellion (Burma), the Gadar Party (Punjab), the Hindustan Republican Association (Uttar Pradesh), Savarkar brothers (Maharastra) etc. Most of the leaders of these movements if not hanged outright were deported to Cellular Jail. Several died due to inhuman treatment and tortures. The horrors of prison life included among many other inhuman forms of torture, flogging on triangular iron frame, bar fetters, cross bar fetters, neck ring shackles, leg iron chains, gang chain, gunny bag uniform, oil grinding, feeble diet, coconut coir rope making, hanging by the leg in the sun, merciless heating and many more. It was the political freedom fighters that first rebelled against the tyranny of the Jailor David Barry.

Political Prisoners in Cellular Jail

The freedom fighters had brought about a pioneering change in the course of life for the British. Much as they wished to subdue the patriots, the undeterred heroes did fear for none. And with enlightened leaders, educated and level-headed to the limit that they could gauge every cunning move of the British, things at times turned worse for the ruling autocrats. They tried to enchain them in the hideous Cellular Jail, just to isolate them from the society and make a mockery of their daily life and radical activities. These revolutionaries were thus convicted for political offence, and Lord Minto, the governor-general of India, in his letter to the provincial governments had referred to these prisoners as 'political prisoners'. But they were never treated so and were denied the privileges as permissible to the political prisoners, as is evident from the government letter of 2nd August 1910, by which the chief commissioner, Andamans was directed not to call them political prisoners as it would 'tend to give them a spurious importance'. In turn, the commissioner in his letter of 9th September 1910 ensured its observance.

David Barrie, head overseer and jailor of the Cellular Jail, did not take the precaution not to call them 'political prisoners', nor did he tolerate the use of this expression by any of his subordinates. "There is none here of that kind", he used to say and he termed them disdainfully as the 'despicable lot', 'vagrant wretches' and 'scum of the society'. They were treated as 'dangerous prisoners' and a badge with the letter 'D' used to hang round the neck of political prisoners. This, however, did not daunt the political prisoners to fight for their due recognition. Hrishikesh Kanjilal and G.D. Savarkar wrote to the Government of India for treating them as political prisoners, but the government in November 1912 informed the superintendent of the jail that "the prisoners should be given clearly to understand that they were not to be considered as political prisoners". Nani Gopal Mukherjee continued a grim battle to get it conceded from the government. Some of the other independent, educated activists included Maulana Fazl-e-Haq Khairabadi, Maulana Ahmadullah, Molvi Abdul Rahim Sadiqpuri, Vinayak Damodar Savarkar, Ganesh Savarkar, Bhai Parmanand, Sohan Singh, Vaman Rao Joshi, Nand Gopal, Ullaskar Dutt, Indubhusan Roy and Barindra Kumar Ghosh.

Although according to the government's instructions, the political prisoners were to be considered as ordinary prisoners, they were actually treated worse than ordinary prisoners from every angle. These educated prisoners were assigned tough manual jobs, whereas ordinary prisoners with meagre knowledge of even the English alphabet were given the light work in the printing press or the work of a munshi (clerk). The ordinary convicts deployed on hard labour were released and promoted as warders and petty officials, which was not in the lot of political prisoners. Any ordinary convict below twenty years of age was not employed on the oil-mill, but a political prisoner of any age was so employed indiscriminately. The political inmates were treated differently even in the jail hospital. An ordinary convict was provided medical attention unlike political prisoners.

They had to walk a distance of five to ten miles, shivering all the while with fever and carrying beds and utensils over their shoulders. Ordinary convicts had the liberty to speak to each other, which was denied to the political prisoners. Ordinary convicts were released from the Cellular Jail after a period of six months and were sent outside for work. But the political prisoners were kept inside the jail for years at a stretch. The privilege of earning remission was not allowed to them. They could never hope to become self-supporting convicts. As life within the jail was quite macabre and unbearable, the political prisoners voiced their desire to work outside, because of comparative diverse facilities. The work was light and the food was better. There was freedom of company and speech. The admission in the hospital outside was much easier compared to the jail hospital. The political inmates fought for it and after the first general strike in the Cellular Jail, some of the political prisoners were sent outside to work. The working outside too became a suffering, as they were at work from 6 to 10 in the morning and 1 to 4.30 in the afternoon. They were harshly exposed to rain and the scorching sun. The workers in the forests faced several other hardships. Their ration was stolen and sold in the villages and medical facilities were denied to them. The outside work proved a delusion and one by one they came back to the dungeon cells to be consumed inside the jail.

The political prisoners were not allowed to communicate with each other. All conversation was illegal and volatile of the "Barrie principle" of administration. The stern Pathan-Jamadar Khoyedad used to keep a check on the interaction between the prisoners. The only opportunity for them to inquire about the health of the co-accused by signal was at a common place, i.e., during the time of bathing at the tank or at meal times, but if any of them was found talking, he was punished with seven days standing handcuffs. The warder was transferred to another section if by civility he conveyed the good wishes of one prisoner to the other. Talking to the authorities about a co-prisoner was also considered an offence for political prisoners. The medical facilities provided were severely inadequate. Common ailments like headache and stomach-ache were reprobated as 'feigning' problems. Political inmates with high temperature were treated while still-locked in their cells. Barrie never permitted the admission of a political prisoner in the jail hospital without his consent. Barrie rather used to threaten the doctor that since he was a Hindu, he should not believe these prisoners and only those persons be considered sick who were so declared by him (Barrie). The political prisoner was not admitted to the hospital till he was actually confined to bed and the doctor declared the prisoner as sick only when he was on his deathbed. If the matter was brought to the notice of higher authorities, Barrie used to label these complaints as 'false allegations' and the chief commissioner believed him and in turn threatened the prisoners with dire punishment if such false allegations were repeated. Nobody in the jail was concerned with the fate of the political prisoners.

Tyranny of David Barry

Indeed the most inhuman jailor David Barry, who posed as if he was destined to suppress the enemies of British rule in India with vile abuse and crude violence. Barinder Kumar Ghosh in his memoirs has given the summary of a short speech delivery by this abominable custodian being a welcome address to the newly arrived prisoners. He said,

> "You see the wall around? Do you know why it is so low? Because it is impossible to escape from this place. The sea surrounds it for a distance of 1000 miles. In the forest you do not find any other animal than pigs and wild cats, it is true, but there are savages who are called Jarawas. If they happen to see any man, they do not hesitate to pierce him right through with their sharp arrows. And do you see me? My name is David Barry. I am the most obedient servant to the simple and straight forward, but to the crooked I am for times as crooked. If you disobey me, may God help you; at least you will know me that am certain. Remember also that God does not come within three miles of Port Blair. The red turbans you see there are warders. And those in black uniforms are petty officers. You must obey them, if they happen to molest you, inform me, I will punish them".[11]

Upendra Nath Bandopadhyay refers to Mr. David Barry as a Bull Dog in appearance who resembled one who was specially created by divine providence to keep prisoners under absolute control. Pointing to the jail building he would say, "It is there we tame lions. You will meet your friend, but mind you, do not talk". Veer Savarkar refers to the familiar address of David Barry in the following words:

> "Listen, ye prisoners, in the Universe there is one God and he lives in Heaven above. But in Port Blair there

> are two, one the God of Heaven and another the God of Earth that is, myself. The God of Heaven will reward you when you go above, but this God of Port Blair will reward you here and now. So ye prisoners, behave well. You may complain to any superior against me but my word shall prevail, I hold my own".[12]

To add insult to injury, Mr. David Barry always tried to create bitterness between the Hindus and the Muslim prisoners. Savarkar referring to his early days in Andamans observed in his celebrated book, *The Story of My Transportation for Life*, "The man who ruled the prison with an iron hand, who made the prisoners tremble in their shoes, could not bear the slight to his authority by political prisoners like us. Even the Jamadars dared pour foul abuse upon us and Mr. David Barry had instigated him to do so. The Jamadars and his lieutenant slapped us on the face if we were found taking or had not finished our day's work. And if we happened to report the incident to the jailor, the later would laugh outright on his face".[13] Savarkar specially mentioned the name of Mirza Khan. He calls him a miniature Barry - jailor. Barin Ghosh has given life-sketches of these smaller gods who ruled the destiny of the political prisoners of the Andamans. "In the Andamans it is they who are in charge of everything and have the authority. They are the bodyguards of the supreme lord, the jailor. And what perfect adopts they are in the art of beating and abusing".[14]

Once a political prisoner named "Bakulla is late in coming from the latrine, apply the baton and unloose the skin of his posterior". Such were the prisons. In fact, the soul crushing indignities and tortures knew no bound under ruthless Mr. Barry. Even the call of nature would need the Jailor's permission who would most often growl, "why the devil did you have it?" Any one who dared to reply would receive slaps in the face. As Veer Savarkar puts it "who can describe the sufferings, these agonies of mind and body". "Here", said Barin Ghosh, "there was no such thing as gentlemen, not even perhaps such a thing as man, here were only convicts".

Plight of Political Prisoners

The lifc of the freedom fighters in the Cellular Jail was one of suffering and humiliation, it was hard and difficult. Filling the swamps, hill cutting, clearing the forest, gardening, husking, making hukka shells, coir pounding and operating oil mills, etc. were the types of manual labour they were subjected to Non compliance with stringent jail regulations attracted severe punishment which included flogging, solitary confinement. All kinds of fetters were used to cause physical inconvenience and mental tortures. A life of torture and humiliation caused such frustration and despair that there were instances of suicide, insanity, illness and deaths. The suicide of Indu Bhusan Roy and Ulaskar Datta revealed the precipice of callousness of the authority in dealing with the political prisoners inside jail. Most of the political prisoners belonging to the intelligentsia were not accustomed to do hard physical labour. Frequently many of them fainted in the process. Only a person with a callous and sound body could hardly complete his daily quota of extracting thirty pounds of coconut oil. Consequently after a few days many of the prisoners fell ill. Some of them pretended illness or deliberately applied dangerous shrubs, roots and berries on the wounds, inflicted by them on their bodies for becoming a patient in the hospital. Others feigned madness. In order to prove that they were really mad, they besmeared their faces with urine and excreta and occasionally ate these dirty things. Food was insufficient and of very bad quality. Moreover the Punjabi and Pathan warders exacted food from political prisoners. If they refused to give food to them they were tortured in several ways by the convict jamadars.

The political prisoners were constantly humiliated by Barry and his subordinates. Barry used to refer them as a despicable lot, vagrant wretches and the scum of the society. The convict warders took a sort of devilish enjoyment in torturing them. In spite of the fact that political prisoners were capable of doing clerical work; they were not employed on it. The privilege of earning remission was not allowed to them. In such circumstances it was quite natural for political prisoners to consider his lot more miserable than life of the seasoned criminal transported to the Andamans. The father of unrest in the Andamans regarded by Craddock and David Barry was Veer Savarkar. Savarkar writes to his brother about the plight of the political prisoners in Cellular Jail:

> "the sentence of picking Oakum was substituted by work round the grinding oil mill... we were to be yoked like animals to the handle that turned the wheel... twenty turns of the wheel were enough to drain away the strength of the strongest coolly and the worst brawny badmash (bad character). No doubt past twenty was put on that work, but the poor political prisoners were fit to do it at any age".[15]

What he and his other fellow political prisoners found most galling was that 'there was no water for washing hands'. Drinking water was even scarce and water for a bath practically unobtainable. Barinder Ghosh has written that at the time of the bath, where they had to stand in line; they were like Draupadi in the assembly of the Kauravas. As regards sanitary arrangements, the less said that better, they were non-existent. The prisoners were allowed out for the purpose only three times a day morning, noon and evening and at no other time, not under any circumstances. Another form of punishment was to harness convicts, instead of horses or bullocks, to the carriages carrying government officials. The *Tribune* went on to state that:

'The regulation about punishment for a short work is that if the prisoners are unable to go though the fill quality of work or fail to turn out the required amount of work they will be handcuffed for a week. This is the punishment for the first offence. For the next offence the punishment is fetters for a month or two, then cross- bars for ten days – a punishment which compels the victim to keep his legs apart- and for further repetition of the offence, fetters for six months or so and solitary confinement'.[16]

Due to heavy discontentment and dissatisfaction, one of the political prisoner sent a letter to India in 1910. The political leaders agitated and criticized the British authority for not complying to the regulations made for this purpose. A commission constituted under the aegis of Lt. Colonel Browning to make enquiry of the charges made in that letter. On the recommendations separate confinement was introduced with the intention to keep the political prisoners separate from each others. It was the political prisoner who first rebelled against the tyranny of the Jailor David Barry. Indeed the tortures inflicted by the jail authorities increased day by day. The political freedom fighters were handcuffed together in pairs and these handcuffs were never opened. The acute discomfort and mental agony that the prisoners had to undergo in attending to the calls of nature, eating, bathing and sleeping can well be imagined. They were punished severely for the slightest lapse in their work.

One such incident worth mentioning about Nand Gopal,[17] A Punjabi Ksharitriya who was sentenced to fourteen years imprisonment for writing seditious articles in his paper *Swaraj* deliberately moved the machine of oil very slowly. As a result of this action his output was much less than the required quota of the day. In the afternoon the warder asked him to finish his lunch in few minutes. But Nand Gopal refused to do so because it was not hygienic to gulp the food so quickly. In the evening he was fettered and confined in the cell. Meanwhile authorities were ordered that every political prisoner should grind oil for three days. This action forced the prisoners to go on a general strike. The jail authorities took rigorous measures to suppress the strike, punishment of invalid diet, fetters and handcuffs for seven days were awarded to them. All of them were confined to cells. Majority of the political prisoners were confined in cells for three months. As a result of the long confinement in solitary cells, some of them fell ill. The authorities adopted the policy if anybody of them fell ill he was not sent to hospital but was returned to solitary confinement.

Around the same time one of the political prisoner named Indu Bhusan committed suicide due to hard punishment and was engaged on the 'Kolhu' (Oil Mill). On account of this hard work he fell ill several times. Whenever he reported about his illness the authorities made fun of him. For pretending illness he was confined to solitary confinement in his cell in chains. Such type of humiliation was beyond the endurance of Indu Bhusan. On April 29, 1912 he committed suicide by hanging himself with a noose made of his own clothes.[18] Soon after the suicide of Indu Bhusan Roy the insanity of Ulaskar Dutt, increased the resentment of political prisoners. He was forced to do hard work under summer mid-day sun to carry bricks for construction. He also exchanged words with his petty officer, who wanted share in his diet. Ulaskar refused to share diet and work. As a punishment he was given three months additional sentence of hard labour. Barrie, the jailor threatened him with a sentence of thirty stripes in case of disobedience of orders in future. Ulaskar Dutt replied to Barrie do whatever he likes. Ulaskar was chained and caused severe pain in the body due to hard work along with tremendous excitement and anger made semi-conscious on June 10, 1923. it was later found that Ulaskar was suffering from fever with a temperature of 107 degrees. The convict warden dragged him from his cell for taking him to the hospital. In hospital the doctor gave him electric shocks. Ulaskar remained unconscious for a number of days. On regaining consciousness Ulaskar made an unsuccessful attempt to commit suicide.

According to Veer Savarkar the first article on the plight of the political prisoners in the Cellular Jail was published in *Bengalee* edited by Surendranath Banerjee. This article was based on a letter clandestinely received by a jail inmate Hotilall Varma. In the issue dated May 3, 1912, the *Tribune* of Lahore gave extracts from the above article in *Bengalee* about the sufferings of political prisoners in the Andamans. Meanwhile the *Amrita Bazar Patrika* also published an article on the subject. In view of the reply to the Chief Commissioner was unable to initiate action against the on-going misbehaviour with political prisoners. The suicide of Indu Bhusan and the insanity of Ulaskar Dutt made the political prisoners desperate. They now decided to resort to open defiance of the authorities. They sent an ultimatum to the jail authorities that unless better arrangements were made for them within a short period they would not work. Their main demands were:

- Proper food;
- Release from hard labour; and
- Freedom to associate with each other.

The authorities locked them in different cells, each separated from the other by 4 or 5 cells in between to prevent them from talking to each others. Some of the inmates were sent to smaller jails in other and far away islands. Nand Gopal and Noni Gopal Mukerjee were sent to Viper Island Jail. After four days Noni Gopal was brought back to the Cellular Jail, because he had commenced a hunger strike in Viper Island. He was forcibly feeded. Gradually all the political prisoners except Nand Gopal ended the strike.

At the same time an article in *Bengalee* charged with high hand and harsh attitude towards the political prisoners in Cellular Jail. Meanwhile, Noni Gopal was persuaded by his fellow inmates to break his 72 days hunger strike. But the jail authorities did not keep their promise as far as Noni Gopal was concerned. Although he was a term convict and a young lad of 18 years at that time he was engaged on hard labour on the oil mill. On his refusal to wash his clothes he was given clothes made of gunny bags. When he refused to wear them these clothes were forcibly sewed upon his body. He tore those cloths in the night. In the morning his hands and feet were put in chains. But during the night he managed to unlock it. On the next morning he was shifted to a solitary cell. When he refused to have a bath, he was bodily lifted stark naked to be washed on the reservoir. The Bhangis rubbed his skin so hard with dry coconut shreds that his skin burnt with ache. He remained naked whole day and night. This was not the end of atrocities inflicted on Noni Gopal. Barry the jailor severely caned him on the pretext that the inmates of jail were planning to go on strike in support of Noni Gopal. Meanwhile, Noni Gopal was demanded the rank of a political prisoner. But the Chief Commissioner office refused to give him the status and Barry directed not to cane Noni Gopal. After this incident he was shifted to District Jail, where he was again commenced his hunger strike. For three days he did not take food and water and also did not speak. After few days he was brought back to Cellular Jail again. As he continued his hunger strike for five or six days more he was forced to inhale milk through the nose. At last Savarkar and others persuaded him to break his hunger strike on October 5, 1913 at the time of the visit of Craddock.[19]

In November 1913 an article on the subject of the treatment of political prisoners in the Andamans appeared in *India* a journal published in London. After describing the events of the hunger strike and the visit of Sir Percy Lukis, the writer of this article regretted that they were not treated as political prisoners or first class misdemeanants, but they were subjected to heavy fetters and coercion. Inhuman conditions, lawlessness, hard labour, invalid diet, and bad weather caused severe illness and deaths. When the tortures inflicted upon them became unbearable, the political freedom fighters made desperate plans for strikes. Two successive strikes in 1913 compelled the British government to announce a number of concessions to the political prisoners, and all those short of a life sentence, were sent back to the mainland India. Then took place what can truly be described as the first recorded hunger strike not only in the Andamans, but also perhaps on the entire Indian Sub-continent. Before we draw a curtain on the first act in the tragic drama of the Cellular Jail concerning the political prisoners, a reference to Colonel Wedge Wood's article entitled "Hell on Earth: Life in the Andamans", published in Daily Herald is important.[20]

The publication of the article created stir in the official circles in India and London. After a prolonged discussion, the government of India decided to send few political prisoners to mainland jails. Before these prisoners could be actually repatriated to the Indian jails, sixteen political prisoners struck work and offered indefinite strike. The main demands of the political prisoners were as follows:

> 'either they should have the privilege of first class prisoners or they should be put in the category of ordinary prisoners, and given all the facilities to the Cellular Jail. Alternatively they should be sent back to serve their terms in the Jails of India where they may enjoy all the facilities of that jail life including reduction of the period of their sentence on certification of good behaviour'.[21]

According to Veer Savarkar, within few days all political prisoners were sentenced to six months imprisonment in chains. Noni Gopal, who was on hunger strike, was forced to stand for one week with chains on his hand and foot. About six or seven political prisoners also went on sympathetic hunger strike with him. Savarkar was also sentenced to stand for two weeks in a framework of letters, this punishment was followed by chains for hands and feet interlinked with a chain between them. In order to stop communication between them, the prisoners were locked up separately. The prisoners now adopted a new device to keep contact with each other. According to Savarkar, the prisoners rang their shackles on feet and manacles on hands on the bars of their doors of their cell in a particular code. Thus the news not only went round through the adjoining rooms but through all the storeys of a nearby block with no risk of warders betraying them.

During the strike the prisoners were taken out for their lunch and instructed not to talk while dining. This intimidation was unbearable and Noni Gopal defied the silence. Immediately Noni Gopal was lifted bodily and locked in his room. Savarkar was not in favour of the hunger strike as he regarded it to be ruinous to the individual as well as to the cause. He was successful in persuading all those prisoners who were on hunger strike to end it, but Noni Gopal was adamant. In order to persuade Noni Gopal, Savarkar started the hunger strike himself. His action perturbed the authorities who exhorted him to break the fast. Savarkar promised them to do so in case he was allowed to talk to Noni Gopal. Barry took him to Noni Gopal's cell. Savarkar took Noni Gopal aside and whispered. 'Do not die like a woman, if you must die, die fighting like a hero. Kill your enemy and then take leave of this world'. Noni Gopal broke his hunger strike but the work strike however continued.

Notwithstanding with the earlier orders, a fresh notification was issued granting several concessions to political prisoners including remission of sentence. Some of them are also repatriated to mainland considering their long pending demand. The prisoners were allowed to cook their own food and some of them were offered light work. Altogether the situation inside jail improved considerably. Savarkar was not allowed any liberty because he was considered ringleader of the revolutionaries and the father of unrest in the Andamans. The outbreak of the first World War in 1914 stirred the jail inmates and some of them volunteered go to the front of war. Lahore Conspiracy case was initiated; about 36 men were sentenced to death and 77 were sentenced to transportation. Meanwhile a large number of revolutionaries were also sentenced for transportation. The political prisoners from both these provinces were transferred to Andamans. In 1915, soldiers who tried to spread sedition in the army at Rangoon were also transferred to the Andaman. During 1915 – 1916 a large number of political prisoners were transported from different parts of the country. The prominent were Trailokya Nath Chakravarti, a revolutionary, Bhai Parmanand, a Punjabi professor and prominent leader of Gadar Party and

Ramraksha, a Punjabi Brahmin from Rangoon. The accounts of Parmanand and Trailokya Nath Chakravarti mentioned about the conditions of the political prisoners in Cellular Jail do not materially differ from the description of Barin Ghosh and Veer Savarkar. Ramraksha, a Punjabi Brahmin was not allowed to wear the sacred thread. When his thread was removed by the warders he commenced hunger strike. After a fortnight he was fed through the nose. In this manner a month passed. Due to bad weather, invalid diet and physical torture he developed pain in the chest. Shortly afterwards he suffered from consumption. When he was virtually at death's door Savarkar persuaded him to take food. Unfortunately his life could not be saved and he died. Lala Ram Charan Das too suffered from consumption and insanity in jail.

As the things did not improve materially, the political prisoners discussed threadbare to undertake a strike. But the health of many old political prisoners was delicate. Further the penalties inflicted on them would pose risk to their lives. Considering the situation, Veer Savarkar and his brother and other nationalists did not favour it. Pulin De also told them, 'what's the use of making trouble and thereby incur new penalty? Rather carry on somehow, so, that you may get out of the jail and again serve your motherland'. Inspite of the advice of the moderate senior political prisoners, the young extremists started a regular campaign of civil disobedience. It was decided to pay back the jail authorities in their own way insulated or abused. The prisoners stopped the routine work and started loud protests against the bad and insufficient quality of food and gathered together to obstruct any official beating a prisoner. Handcuffs, fetters, bar fetters and solitary confinement were awarded as penalties to the prisoners. When some Sikh prisoners, who were more than fifty years of age, suffered the tortures heroically. Amar Singh is one who was scolded by the jailor, when he resisted, he was punished severely for three months. Parmanand, a young man was abused by Barry. He rushed forward and was lifted with the help of Ashutosh Lahiri. Barry fell on ground. They were awarded twenty strips each as punishment. Both of them suffered flogging unperturbed although their bodies were a mass of lacerated flesh. Similar suffering too was experienced by Bhan Singh. Bhan Singh was mercilessly beaten by a warder, because he returned abuses in full measure to Barry. As a result Bhan Singh vomitted blood, before other political prisoners could rush to his rescue. Few days later, Bhan Singh died in hospital. This incident shocked the entire circle of jail inmates and then called for general strike. On the suggestion of Savarkar a memorandum was submitted demanding immediate action against David Barry. Infact, the memorandum was rejected, leading to strike. Sardar Sohan Singh a sixty years old Sikh and Prithvi Singh, a Punjabi youngman were kept in the cell for few days without a morsel of food. Savarkar persuaded them to strike off the agitation, but Prithvi Singh continued it for two weeks more.[22]

In spite of repeated requests from the beginning, the Sikh prisoners were not given soap for cleaning their long hair and beards. They could also not bear the harsh treatment of warders. Infuriated by this constant humiliation one day Chatter Singh attacked the Jail Superintendent, who rolled the chair. Before any harm could be done to the officer Chatter Singh was overpowered by the petty officials who gave him a sound thrashing. For a number of years he was kept in a cage. Numerous such incidents occurred inside the jail crossing all limits, inflicting pain to the political prisoners. In view of the prolonged trouble in jail, the government of India instructed the Superintendent to treat the political prisoners more leniently and give desk work to them. This action satisfied the political prisoners for the time being. The publication of the news of the strike of political prisoners and the death of Ramraksha and Bhan Singh increased the indignation of the public in India.

Finally the Indian Jail Committee was appointed in 1919 to investigate the whole system of prison administration in

India. The members of the committee visited Cellular Jail in 1920. The political prisoners allowed to submit their grievances. On receipt of the petitions from different jail inmates, the Jails committee extended some relief to prisoners including keeping sacred thread and their symbol of religion on their body. After taking stock of the situation that prevailed in jail, the Jail Committee recommended the abolition of deportation of prisoners to the Kala Paani. The announcement was proclaimed in the Legislative Assembly on March 11, 1921 to abolish the penal settlement altogether. The decision that political prisoners would not be transported to Andamans in future led to the belief that there would be an end of the system of transportation of political prisoners to Port Blair. Meanwhile there was a general demand all over India for the release of the political prisoners in the Andamans. The National Union of Bombay submitted a petition demanding their release. This petition was campaigned and signed by about 70,000 people. The main factor in influencing the Government of India to grant a general amnesty to political prisoners was their desire to facilitate the working of the new reforms incorporated in the Government of India Act of 1919. By 1921, most of the political prisoners were either released or repatriated to the mainland. Around the same time Savarkar too was released by signing a pledge of abstinence from current politics. With this phase, the story of humiliation of Kala Pani ended.[23]

Suspension of Deportation to Andaman Islands

The regular custom of the British to send away the Indians to Kala Paani and their further destruction in the merciless hands of the autocrats had suddenly come to a stop. The Indian Jails Committee was formed in this regard, and a team had paid a visit to the Andaman jail. The members, after much ponderings and discussions came to the final conclusion that their jail rules must be revised. As a result, the deportation to the doomed place was terminated forever. According to the rulers, the penal settlement established there was not up to the mark with their plans, and the inmates needed to be repatriated back to the country. However, a significant amount of prisoners were still lodged there, who were brought back later. The Indian Jails Committee (1919-20) was established by the Government of India on 28th April 1919 to investigate the entire system of jail administration in India, especially the penal settlement in the Andaman. Sir Alexander Cardew, member, Executive Council, Madras was its chairman. Sir James H. Duboulay, secretary, Government of India, Home Department; Col. James Jackson, inspector general of prisons, Bombay; Lt. Col. Sir Walter J. Buchanan, inspector general of prisons, Bengal; Khan Bahadur Khalifa Syed Hamid Hussain, Delhi; D.M. Dorai Rajah of Puddukottah, Madras and Norman G. Mitchell-Innes Esq. inspector of prisons, Home Office, London, were the other members.

The committee visited the Andamans in January 1920 and the report was also submitted in the same year, but it was published only in 1921. The committee was not contented with the working of the penal settlement in the Andaman and accordingly, was in favour of the abandonment of the Andaman as a special place for criminal detention. However, it recommended the preservation of the Andaman as a place of deportation for a restricted class of prisoners whose removal from British India was considered by the government concerned to be in the interest of the public. Unifying the two views, the committee recommended that expatriation to the Andaman should be closed down except with regard to such prisoners as the Governor General-in-Council may, by special or general order direct. The recommendations of the Jails Committee regarding the abolition of the penal settlement were largely accepted by the Government of India. An announcement was made by Sir William Vincent, the Home member in the Legislative Assembly, on 11th March 1921 to the effect that the Government of India had decided to put an end to the use of Andaman as a penal settlement.

As a result, further deportation to the Andamans was discontinued and repatriation started in 1921. Veer Savarkar, G.D. Savarkar and some other political prisoners who were only about thirty in number left in the Cellular Jail by that time, were repatriated to India in 1921. On 23rd September 1922, Sir William Vincent also introduced the Abolition of the Transportation Bill in the Legislative Assembly and informed the house that it was not only the intention of the government to abolish the punishment of deportation, but also to abandon the Andaman, as a penal settlement. The repatriation of other convicts also continued. In 1921 when the government decided to close down the settlement, the convict population in the Andaman was 11,532, but by December 1925 their number was reduced to 7740. The Government of India issued a resolution (No. F-20/26 dated the 27th February 1926) on the subject. However, contrary to the declared policy of the British government, some political prisoners were sent to the Andaman from 1922 onwards till the policy was eventually revised in 1932. The political prisoners deported during this period have been listed in the Andaman and Nicobar Administration release as Lakshmi Kanta Shukla and Vishnu Saran Dublis from the United Province and Kotaya Korrabu, Pandu Padal Bonangi, Sanyasayya Golivilli, Sanyasi Kunchatti, Satyanarayan Raju and Virayya Dora Taggi from Madras. Vishnu Saran Dublis was convicted in the Kakori Conspiracy Case on 6th April 1927. He was sentenced to ten years rigorous imprisonment and was lodged in Naini Central Jail. He was erroneously implicated there in a jail riot case and was sentenced to another term of five years. In all, he was to endure a sentence for fifteen years. He was sent to the Andamans. Lakshmi Kanta Shukla was sentenced to transportation for life for trying to kill a British commissioner of Jhansi. He was sent off to the Andamans. His wife Basumati also accompanied him.

Deportation of Revolutionaries (1932-1938) to Andaman Islands

A special session of the Indian National Congress was held in Calcutta on 4th September 1920 under the presidentship of Lala Lajpat Rai in which a proposal of non-violent non-cooperation was put up by Mahatma Gandhi, with the assurance that if the people followed his advice, he would get them Swaraj within one year. The people responded to it. Even the revolutionaries, despite their dissimilar ideologies, joined the national mainstream wholeheartedly in the peaceful non-cooperation movement. However, the abrupt withdrawal of this movement by Gandhi after the Chauri Chaura incident on 5th February 1922 shocked them all. The revolutionaries again marshalled their secret organisations and started recruiting youth, acquiring money and weapons to fight the ultimate battle with the ruling British. Led by Sachindernath Sanyal, who after his release from the Cellular jail in 1920 was leading a settled married life in U.P and Jogesh Chandra Chatterji, they floated the 'Hindustan Republican Association'. Significant revolutio-naries like Ram Prasad Bismil of Shahjahanpur, Ashfaquallah, Rajinder Lahiri, Chandra Shekhar Azad, Manmathnath Gupta and other devoted workers joined the association. Bejoy Kumar Sinha and Bhagat Singh were also closely associated with it. Its constitution was also framed. In January 1925, they distributed a pamphlet 'Revolutionary' throughout the country, propagating revolution. Signed by Vijay Kumar, president Central Council of the Party, it distinguished 'terrorism' and 'anarchism' from revolution.

In Punjab, Lahore was once again agog with revolutionary activities and Bhagat Singh who was to become Shaheed-i-Azam in subsequent years was on the forefront. All the revolutionary groups from United Provinces, Punjab, Rajputana, and Bengal held a meeting in Feroze Shah Kotla grounds Delhi on 8 and 9 September 1928 which was attended by all important revolutionaries, including Bhagat Singh, Batukeshwar Dutt, Bejoy Kumar Sinha, Jatinder Nath

Dass, Yashpal, Chander Shekhar Azad, Bhagwati Charan Vohra, Rajguru and Mahabir Singh. They rechristened the party as 'Hindustan Socialist Republican Association'. Another wing, the 'Hindustan Socialist Republican Army' was also formed with Chander Shekhar Azad as its chief commander.

The political developments took a speedy turn. On 30th October 1928, Lala Lajpat Rai was leading a huge procession towards the Lahore railway station, to protest against the arrival of 'Simon Commission'. The police resorted to lathi charge and the baton blows hurled on Lala Lajpat Rai caused grave injuries on his body. It was protested vociferously in public. As a result of the chest injuries he suffered, he breathed his last on 17th November 1928 and joined the ranks of the martyrs. It spread a blanket of gloominess throughout the country. The revolutionaries instantly raised an avenging slogan, Khoon ka badla khoon, (blood for blood). The political atmosphere was surcharged throughout the country. The revolutionaries planned to kill Scott, superintendent of police, Lahore. On 17th December 1928, exactly one month after the martyrdom of Lala Lajpat Rai, J.R. Saunders an assistant superintendent of police was shot dead near the SP's office and the D.A.V College, Lahore. Jai Gopal, Raj Guru, Bhagat Singh, Chander Shekhar Azad and Sukhdev carried out this mission and made a successful escapade. This gutsy act bewildered the authorities beyond measure. Revolutionary activities continued in full vitality.

From 1930 to 1933, in Bengal alone, twenty-three officials were killed and thirty-six were injured by the freedom fighters. Forty-seven murderous attempts, 167 attempts of robberies, 16 cases of bomb-throwing and 8 cases of bomb explosion by the revolutionaries took place in that province during that period. The government resorted to tyrannical measures. Special Tribunals were set up by the provincial governments. The Bengal government requested the Government of India to allow them to deport the political prisoners to the Andaman and Nicobar Islands, despite the recommendations of the Prison Reform Committee to the contrary. In May 1932, Sir John Anderson visited the islands and recommended the use of the unnerving penal settlement in view of the relaxed discipline in the Indian jails. The primary complaint of the provincial governments was that the 'terrorists' communicated with terrorist organisations outside, they did not observe jail discipline which had polluted the criminal convicts also, and that they attracted the press for their publicity. The Government of India decided to postpone the implementation of the recommendations of the Committee regarding the abolition of the penal settlement. On 12th July 1932, Sir Samuel Hoare, the secretary of state for India, announced in the House of Commons his approval to the proposal of the Government of India to transfer to the Andamans one hundred convicted 'terrorists'. The policy decision of sending political prisoners to the horrendous 'Kala Paani' was strongly criticised by the public and the press, as it was against the spirit of the report of the Indian Jails Committee, 1919 (Cardew Committee) and their declared policy of abolishing the punishment of deportation. The monstrous gates of Cellular Jail were again waiting for the political prisoners to devour them up.

A batch of twenty-five political prisoners from Bengal including those convicted in the Chittagong Armoury Raid Case was the first to be transferred to the Andamans on 15th August 1932. Some more political prisoners were sent thereafter in 1932 and by the time of the hunger strike in April 1933, the number of political prisoners in the Cellular Jail was approximately one hundred. According to B.K. Sinha, Kamalnath Tewari, Batukeshwar Dutt, Mahabir Singh, Kundan Lal and Dr. Gaya Prasad, all prisoners of Lahore Conspiracy Case were deported to the Andamans in January 1933. Jai Dev Kapoor, Bejoy Kumar Sinha and Sheo Verma reached the Andamans in June 1933. Fresh batches of political prisoners, whether lifers or short-term convicts, were sent to Port Blair thereafter. The political prisoners included not only those charged with murder or attempt to murder or convicted for dissemination of revolutionary ideology, but also those punished in minor criminal cases of political nature. They were all sent off to the Andamans in large numbers.

Political prisoners convicted in Mechuabazar Bomb Case (Calcutta), Mymensingh attack on Ganja Liquor Warehouses, violent attack on Jhansi Commissioner, Armenian Street Political Dacoity, Atharabari Political Dacoity, Arms Act, Sialdah Political Dacoity, Alipore Political Dacoity, Barisal District School Political Dacoity, Faridpur Arms and Explosives Conspiracy, violent attack on Dhaka commissioner, Barisal Conspiracy Case, Brahanbaria Political Dacoity, Dhaka Political Dacoity, Charmaguria Post Office Dacoity, Aranyapasha Arms and Explosives Conspiracy, Dhol Ghat Encounter, Tangail Political Dacoity, Calcutta Arms Possession, Kulaseni Political Dacoity, Damodia Mail Robbery, violent attack on the Statesman Editor, Angaria Mail Robbery, Hill Railway Station Political Dacoity, Manikganj Mail Dacoity, Itkhola Mail Dacoity, Midnapore District Magistrate Murder Conspiracy, Naldanga Political Dacoity, violent attack on police informer, Badhua Political Dacoity, conspiracy to murder Bengal governor, Dinajpore Conspiracy, Birbhum Conspiracy, violation of Internment Order, Inter-Provincial Conspiracy, Gaibandha-Rangapur Arms Conspiracy, Alipur Conspiracy and in many more cases were also sent to the Andamans.

By the end of 1934, the number of political prisoners in the Andaman jail had gone up to 200. It is significant to note that although the sanction for deportation to the Andamans was originally restricted to one hundred prisoners only, political prisoners were deported indiscriminately without observing any constraint. On 14th February 1935, the Home member of the Government of India stated in the Legislative Assembly that the total number of prisoners sent to the Andamans, after having been convicted of crimes connected with terrorism was 237 (208 from Bengal, 13 from Bihar and Orissa, 7 from Punjab, 6 from Madras and 3 from Delhi). In

October 1936, during the time of the visit of Raizada Hans Raj M.L.A. and Mohammad Yamin Khan, M.L.A. to Port Blair, the number of political prisoners in the Cellular Jail had gone up to 310. At one time, the number of political prisoners in. the Andaman jail had still exceeded, although by July 1937 their number had come down to 300, as some of them were repatriated due to illness or on the completion of their sentence. As per the list of political prisoners published by the Ex-Andaman Political Prisoners Fraternity Circle, 332 political prisoners from Bengal, 9 from U.P., 3 from Punjab, 18 from Bihar, 1 from Delhi, 3 from Madras and in all 366 were sent to the Andamans from 1932 to 1938.

Last Phase: Milestone History

The recrudescence of the revolutionary enterprises throughout India led to reconsidering opening of Andaman Islands for deportation for hard core political prisoners to curtail further communication among the agencies. The hell on earth once again was put under practice to bring necessary political discipline. The last batch of political prisoners including the heroes of the Chittagong Armoury Raid case was deported to the Andamans during 1932-38. They consisted of 366 freedom fighters of which 332 were from Bengal alone. This was the most turbulent period in the Cellular Jail marked by two fast-unto-death hunger strikes. The political prisoners decided to offer resistance from the beginning; otherwise their troubles would go on increasing day by day. They also decided to uphold the tradition of resistance offered by the earlier batches of political prisoners. As Bijoy Kumar Sinha stated that the conditions inside jail were as they were earlier or even worst. The dilapidated condition with crevices in the walls everywhere, the roofs of the cells leaked in the torrential rains which were frequent in the tropical islands, bad food, which even sometimes contained worms, lack of medical aid, insufficient drinking water, hard task like coir pounding, callous and discourteous behaviour of the jail authorities, unsanitary conditions of the cell, in recreational including library facility and the sufferings were innumerable. As said regarding this batch most of them were highly educated and belonging to middle class families and influenced by Marxist philosophy.

Communist Consolidation, Indian Extremist Organisation

Communist Consolidation is regarded as an Indian communist organisation. This establishment was formed by the prisoners of the Andaman Cellular Jail. 39 inmates of the jail established this organisation on 26th April 1935. The founding members were initially associated with the pro-Marxist section of the Anushilan Samiti. A bulk of the countrywide Anushilan marxist inclination however did not trust the Communist Party enough to join it. Communist Consolidation initiated in organising a May Day celebration in 1935. They started publishing a hand-written magazine, *The Call*.

Shortly, membership of the Organisation expanded to nearly 200-500. Shiv Verma (an associate of Bhagat Singh, later became CPI(M) leader in Uttar Pradesh), Hare Krishna Konar (later became a founding leader of CPI(M)), Biplabi Dhrubesh Chattopadhyay (who was sentenced to 7 years imprisonment as he was found guilty in connection with the Dakhineswar Bomb Case), Ananta Chakravorty (a Jugantar party member, also sentenced for the Conspiracy and Bomb Case), Nalini Das (a Jugantar party member, sentenced for the Mechua Bazar Bomb Case), Fakir Sen and Jibendra Das (an Anushilan revolutionary from Tripura) were the praiseworthy members of the Communist Consolidation group.

Hunger Strikes

The political prisoners started agitating against the barbaric and inhuman behaviours of the jail authorities. There were a number of strikes and hunger strikes, but there was no improvement on their plight. On the contrary the jail administration started crushing political prisoners with an iron rod. The political freedom fighters resorted to different methods of defiance and resistance to protest against the British tyranny. Ultimately, a hunger strike was declared on May 12, 1933. The agitation lasted for 46 hours. During the first hunger strike on May 1933 the authorities resorted to the customary force-feeding by stout ruffian convicts, which resulted in the death of three precious lives of martyrs – Mahabir Singh of the Lahore Conspiracy case, Mohit Mitra convicted under Arms Act and Mohan Kishore Monodas also under Arms Act.[24]

The martyrdom of three political prisoners viz., Mahabir Singh, Mohit Mitra and Mohan Kishore Monodas, within a short period in the Cellular Jail increased the resentment of the people in India. This issue was raised in the Central Legislative Assembly and other forums deemed fit demanded redressal immediately. The strike was called off on June 26, 1933 and political prisoners were allowed to mix among themselves and provided with study materials, newspapers and books. Four years later the second mass hunger strike began and this time, the prisoners demanded immediate repatriation to the mainland. To give relief the jail authorities instructed to maintain decorum of jail norms. The conditions were improved and the curteous and soft behaviour resumed only for few days. In 1934, 535 rebels sentenced to transportation in the Thrawardy Rebellion case in Burma were sentenced to Andamans. With the induction of new group, the jail authorities withdrew the facilities extended to them on the pretext of contamination and communication among the political prisoners. Meanwhile the request of old political prisoners to meet the new batch was not accepted. This led to differences with the jail authorities and gradual rift caused disturbances. Indeed the first kind of non-cooperation movement was observed by the political prisoners and boycotted all the orders issued by the jail authorities.

In spite of the gloomy prospects of suffering and death, the spirit of the political prisoners was buoyed up with the course of political events in India which they had followed closely during the years through whatever books and newspapers made available to them. They knew that Indian National Congress and other political parties were consistently raising their repatriation and early release. The mass hunger strike by 177 political prisoners was commenced on July 1937, which lasted for 36 days. They, who were very serious about their resolve to die for a cause, stuck all along to their determination of not eating voluntarily were on fast unto death. In spite of all the efforts of the jail authorities, the number of serious cases among the strikers increased day by day. Another difficulty faced by the jail authorities was the refusal of the criminal convicts to join the feeding gang. Virtually the situation became worst and worst. The second hunger strike resulted in the death of Indu Bhusan Rai, Ram Rakha and Kehar Singh and many others lost their health and mental balance. Nevertheless the British administration remained unmoved. Perhaps they thought that the cry of the political prisoners will remain confined to the four walls of the Cellular Jail and even its echoes would be lost in the roaring waves of the sea all around. They were greatly astonished when despite the strict watch on the political prisoners, they were able to send to the mainland tales of their woes and sufferings. Indeed this news created tremendous uproar in the entire country. In their sympathy and support, the other freedom fighters undergoing imprisonment in different jails of the country, also started hunger strikes. One such support for their demand grew countrywide and political prisoners at Alipore, Deoli, Behrampur and other innumerable jails of India too went on hunger strike on August 10, 1937 demanding the redressal of the grievances of the political prisoners in the 'Kala Paani' within twenty four hours.[25]

The 1937 hunger strike stirred the soul of the nation. Poet Rabindranath Tagore and Mahatma Gandhi became restless.

'We cannot allow these flowers of the nation to wither away' said Tagore. On 28 August 1937 Mahatma Gandhi and the Congress Working Committee sent a telegram "The whole nation appeals to you to end the hunger strike... and assures you to take up your demands and to see them fulfilled". After this, a lot of deliberations and discussions were held and finally the historic 36-day hunger strike of 200 revolutionary freedom fighters ended on August 28, 1937.[26] Ultimately the Government was compelled to repatriate all political prisoners to the mainland and by January 1938 the Cellular Jail was denuded of all these freedom fighters. With their departure the chapter of the sufferings of political freedom fighters from India in the 'Kala Paani' ended. Like all other historic landmarks in the Indian Freedom Struggle, the Cellular Jail generated mixed reactions and stands in the midst of Indian freedom struggle. The hundred years of struggle and sacrifices brought laurels to Andamans. Indeed the sufferings of the freedom fighters in dark, damp and dingy thickly Cellular Jail cells, brought glory to the nation.

Demolition of Cellular Jail

The Japanese occupied the Islands in March 1942. A hell of terror was let loose by the Japanese during the three and a half years of their occupation of the islands and hundred of islanders were tortured and many shot dead on the mere plea of spying for the British. Meanwhile the Japanese had partly demolished two wings of the Cellular jail; whereas free India demolished two more to construct Gobind Ballabh Pant Hospital. Subash Chandra Bose visited the Jail in December 1943 and hoisted the National Flag before the rest of the country become free.

REFERENCES

1. It is believed that the year 1858 to 1860 some 2000 to 4000 rebels from different parts of the country were deported to Andamans from the ports viz., Calcutta, Karachi and Madras. Mazumder. R.C., *Penal settlement in Andamans*, Ministry of Information and Publicity, Government of India, New Delhi, 1975. p. 142.

2. *Ibid.*, p. 233.
3. Aparna Vaidik, Settling the convicts : Matrimony and Domesticity in the Andamans, *Studies in History*, Vol. XXII, No-2, New Delhi, July-December 2006. p. 221.
4. Legislative Assembly Proceedings, May 28, 1933, National Archives of India, New Delhi.
5. Savarkar convicted in Nasik Conspiracy case (December 1910) was sentenced to Andaman for fifty years of imprisonment.
6. He was also convicted in what is known as the Nasik Conspiracy case.
7. Nani Gopal Mukherjee had been sentenced for having thrown a bomb on the car of a high police dignitary. He was 16 years old. Prison regulations did not allow anyone of so tender an age to be put on hard labour. He was on hunger strike for 72 days.
8. Bhai Paramanand was sentenced to death in the Lahore Conspiracy case - the sentence was commuted to transportation to the Andamans - was a guest of honour on the occasion of the inauguration of the Cellular Jail as a National Memorial on February 11, 1979 at Port Blair.
9. He was a founder member of the Gadar party. Sentenced to death in the Lahore case in 1915. Afterwards commuted to life imprisonment and deported to Cellular Jail – Andaman. In his famous book *'Kranti Path Ke Pathik'*, mentioned about the tortures, atrocities and humiliation caused to the freedom fighters in Andaman.
10. A redoubtable revolutionary leader, transported to the Andamans in 1916.
11. *Ibid.*, p. 194.
12. *Ibid.*
13. Mukherji. Dr. S.K., *Islands of India*, Ministry of I & B, GOI, New Delhi, 1992. p. 135.
14. Iqbal Narain, *The Andaman Story*, Vikas Publications, New Delhi, 1978. p. 193.
15. *Ibid*. p. 194.
16. *Ibid*. p. 198.
17. Mathur. L.P., *Kala Pani*, Eastern Book Corporation, Delhi. 1985. pp. 76-77.
18. Home Department, Political Branch, B Procedings,No. 1, July 1912, Natioanl Archives of India, New Delhi.

19. Mazumder. R.C., *op.cit.*, pp. 189-91.
20. Home Department, Political Branch, Deposit Proceedings, January 1921, National Archives of India, New Delhi.
21. Home Department, Political Branch, A proceedings Nos. 68-460. February 1915, National Archives of India, New Delhi.
22. Savarkar. V.D., (1950) *The story of My Transportation for Life* (A Biography of Black Days in the Andamans) (Translated from the original in Marathi by Y.N. Naik), Sadhaakti Publications, Bombay.
23. Tamta. B.R., (1992) *Andaman and Nicobar Islands*, National Book Trust, New Delhi. pp. 30-31.
24. After four weeks telegrams from Bengal's chief ministers, leaders of the nation Jawaharlal Nehru, Subash Chandra Bose, Sharad Chandra Bose and other leaders poured in imploring the freedom fighters to end the hunger strike. *Ibid.*, p. 35.
25. Sinha. Bijoy Kumar, *In Andamans, the Indian Bastille*, Swastika Agencies, Calcutta, pp. 46-53.
26. Mathur. L.P., (1969) *History of the Andaman and Nicobar Islands* (1756-1966), Sterling Publishers, New Delhi. p. 125.

4
Intellectual Culling—A clandestine Strategy of Colonial State in Andaman Islands

It had repeatedly been said that many Englishwomen had been dishonoured; this was said on the floor of British Parliament again and again. Marx disbelieved such inflammatory rumours with remarkable prescience, as may be seen through an article of his in *New York Tribune*, 15 April 1858. After the rebellion was suppressed, despite the English assiduously trying to find evidence against the Rebels for molesting English women nothing by way of evidence could be found. Yet the cry that "the natives have dishonoured our women", was a very important piece of hate propaganda spread in England against the Mutineers and used to justify all barbarities perpetrated.

Even before they could have possibly known of the Kanpur massacre that took place later, the English had begun committing atrocities on Indian men, women and children. Let us hear what J.W. Kaye, says about the haunting dilemma that British atrocities posed for him. "An English man is almost suffocated with indignation when he reads that Mrs. Chambers or Miss Jennings were hacked to death by a dusky ruffian. But in native histories, or history being wanting in native legends and traditions, it may be recorded against our people, that mothers, wives and children with less familiar names, fell miserable victims to the first swoop of English vengeance, and these stories may have as deep a pathos as any that rend our own hearts".

Such atrocities undertaken by the English from the beginning of the Mutiny enflamed the rebels and hardened their hearts. The English gave no quarter to their opponents: As Engels recalled in 1870 they violated all laws of war in killing the prisoners of war; and they did so by ever imaginable, fiendish means, like hanging after binding their victims in contorted forms or — a special favourite — blowing the captives from mouths of their guns. Right from the beginning, with Col. James Neill's expedition in early June 1857 horrible bouts of atrocities were committed by the British as they regained each village or town from the rebels. There was a frenzied general massacre of civilians at Delhi upon its fall in September 1857, devastating and de-peopling the whole city, an account of which may be read in William Dalrymple's, *Last Mughal*. Every subsequent success of the British was similarly marked by a general massacre and plunder of civil populations. William Russell of *London Times* was a witness to the British loot of Lucknow in March 1858. A Maharashtrian pilgrim caught in the rebellion similarly described the slaughter of civilians, including women and children, wrought by the British at Jhansi and neighbouring places. The repression continued even after the end of the rebellion. There were pursuits, trials and executions. Confiscations of land and properties followed. Not only individual rebels but whole families, whose members were suspected of having been involved in any way in the Mutiny were deprived of their lands. The confiscated lands were given to British families and to such 'natives' as could claim to have rendered service against their own compatriots.

The defeat of the Rebellion of 1857 seemed at the time total, and as a consequence, the repressive and exploitative nature of British rule now appeared in a still more naked form. And yet even in its defeat, the Revolt weakened the capacity of British imperialism to continue with its policy of territorial aggrandizement, since it could no longer rely on Indian troops for external adventures. Before 1857 there were over 2,00,000 Indian sepoys in the three Presidency Armies. This number had been reduced to 1,21,000 by 1862-63, while the number of European soldiers in India was increased from 38,000 to 76,000 — so that there was now one European soldier to watch over every two Indian sepoys! Moreover Indians were excluded from the Artillery branch. Since, a European soldier's pay was several times that of an Indian, the burden of military expenditure fell even more heavily on the Indian tax-payer's shoulders. Yet the army was far less effective. Thus the grand designs of British imperialism which had been based on the use of Indian troops as cannon fodder, could no longer be pursued with the same élan. To this extent the 1857 Rebellion helped to shield other Asian nations from British onslaughts for a long time.

Bahadur Shah, the last Mughal king, is not one of the heroic figures of the Revolt of 1857. But he was a poet, and as he was being tried, deprived of pen and paper, he scrawled with charcoal on the walls of his cell, verses of sorrow and sadness at the tragic end of the Great Rebellion. The bulk of the verses translated below belong to a poem that was already being sung by "the minstrels of India", according to a report of the Political Agent of Bhopal, dated 14 June 1862.

> "The way the wind has changed so suddenly and totally, my heart now knows no quiet.
>
> How can I recount that tale of cruelty, for my breast is shattered by sorrow?
>
> How have the people of India been destroyed! What cruelties have been perpetrated on them!
>
> Whomever the victorious masters saw, they said,
>
> 'He is fit enough for the gallows.'
>
> No one buried the dead under the earth, no one gave them a shroud,
>
> They could never attain their native place, nor is there any sign anywhere of their graves."
>
> "Friends, I am that slaughtered man, at whose corpse,

a whole world will continue to look with grief and envy.

O Zafar, so long as the country of India endures,

the star of the glory of this flower will ever shine."

The last lines contained a proud boast on behalf of the rebel dead. It is for the people of India to show more than hundred and fifty years later, how much they care for the memory of those who died so bravely for her.

British Atrocities in Andaman

The Andaman Islands was mute witness of crime by the imperialist foreign power to suppress the freedom movement of India. Nonetheless, the entire penal servitudes were much more disgraceful and shameful. Newton's third law is bound to have its effect and the perpetrators of the crime would be made to pay for their misdeeds with compound interest. With the introduction of various aspects which led to the consolidation of the Andaman Islands, the actual construction of the road becomes a topic in its own right. The work involved was very different to our present day road building techniques. The effort put into the operations was very labour intensive and all the manual work on the islands was performed by convicts, mostly those who had committed further crimes in the colony after arrival were given harder works. Sometimes they have to work twelve to fourteen hours a day and if failed to do so they were given extra punishment like washing clothes and cleaning utensils. Arduous manual labour in the form of oil-grinding, coir-making or rope-making was accompanied by regular beatings for inmates.

The tasks for which convicts confined in the Cellular Jail could be employed were: 1. Cane and bamboo work; 2. Coconut and mustard oil mills; 3. Husking and opening coconuts; 4. Drying copra; 5. Making hooka shells; 6. Coir pounding; 7. Sisal pounding; 8. Rope making; 9. Net making; 10. Carpet making; 11. Weaving towels; 12. Coir and sisal hemp mat making; 13. Cleaning mustard seeds; 14. Blanket mulling; 15. Gardening; 16. Hill cutting and swamp filling in (when necessary); 17. Miscellaneous, such as conservancy, cleaning drains etc., around the jail; 18. Miscellaneous lowly duties in connection with the jail like hospital ward coolies, sweeping etc., and, 19. Clerical work in the jail office.

There were, however rules and regulations for assignment of manual labour to the prisoners. Prisoners below twenty years of age could not be assigned arduous manual labour; literates were employed in the press and the work was assigned according to the physical fitness of the prisoners. Political prisoners were treated differently. They were assigned grueling manual labour and under the well-determined plan, abuses and humiliations were hurtled upon them deliberately to reduce them to mental and physical wrecks. The most torturous and backbreaking labour was assigned to these political prisoners. Many of them hailed from cultured and educated 'Bhadralok' (well-to-do) families. The coir-pounding, rope-making, oil grinding in the mills were some of the severest tasks to which they were employed. The specific quota of each job was fixed and anybody who could not complete it during the determined time had to dispense with his sleep in order to accomplish the task. Even illness was taken as 'feigning' in the case of these 'dangerous' convicts.

On arrival in the Andamans, the convicts were also given the rigorous labour of coir pounding. The beating of dry and hard remains of coconut shells daylong and day after day caused massive swelling on the palms. It led to injuries on the hands and bleeding. When he showed his injured hands to the superintendent of the jail and requested him to change his assignment he was deputed to the oil-mill, a still harder job. Once the fibres were ready, ropes were made by another batch, i.e. by those who were given the light labour. Each had to turn out 3 lbs. weight of ropes. Letters and manuals also explain the rigour of the hard manual labour involved in rope-making, and how the degrading orders were passed by the warders. Although rope-making (technically called picking oakum) was also a difficult task, but the good thing was the company of prisoners working in the same chawl and this mode of working was a consolation to them. The coir-making groups, talking to each other during work, was looked upon as 'kindness of the jail authorities' and the political prisoners were isolated for such a duty after an officer from Calcutta visited the Andamans, and warned the authorities against such 'facilities' being given to the political prisoners. The work of picking oakum was also substituted by work on the oil-mill. Oil-grinding was the hardest labour and was described in the memoirs of all the political prisoners who were sent to the Andamans as the cause of greatest misery. There were two processes of working the oil-grinding mill in the Cellular Jail. One was like the system followed by the oil men in India in which bullocks were yoked to the handle of the mill and they moved round it continuously; only in this case, the political prisoners were substituted for the bullocks. In the other process, the handle was moved by the hand of the prisoner who had to run round and round the mill. In both the cases, the prisoners were to work until 30 lbs. of coconut oil or 10 lbs. of mustard oil was produced. In order to demoralize the spirit the cellular jail gave them hard work to do for two months continuously, then one month on picking oakum and again the grinding work on the mill.

The inmates had to sit down from sheer exhaustion and helplessness. Ordinarily, all work had to be stopped between ten and twelve. But this Kohlu, as the oil mill labour was referred to, had to continue throughout. The door was opened only when the meal was announced. The man came in and served the meal in the pan and went away and the door was shut. If after washing his hands one were to wipe away the perspiration of his body, the jamadar-the worst of gangsters in the whole lot-would go at him. If the prisoners were unable to go through the stipulated labour, they were handcuffed for a week. This was the punishment for the first offence. For the second offence a week's handcuffs and four-day starvation diet. For the next offence, the punishment was fetters for a month or two, followed by cross-bars for ten days-punishment which compelled the victim to keep his legs apart - and for further repetition of the offence, fetters for six months or so and solitary confinement were awarded. All these penalties were inflicted upon the political prisoners very often.

According to the jail rules, the work of the prisoner was not to be checked in the first fifteen days of his arrival in the jail. This rule was however gladly violated in the case of the political prisoners. According to the rules, after the expiry of three months of continuous hard labour, the prisoners were to be deployed on light work for the next three months. But asking for light work was always denied. Ashutosh Lahiri, an inmate of the Cellular, was struck off the work. He was punished and was awarded thirty floggings with contemptible ill will. The convicts in the martial law cases on their arrival in Cellular Jail were allotted oil mill grinding which they refused in pursuance of the policy of Satyagraha adopted by the political prisoners.

The abnormal rate of sickness and death among the prisoners was due to the severe weather of the islands. The poor and unhygienic food coupled with hard work could lead anyone to illness. The prisoners were not given medical aid and many of them contracted dangerous diseases and died due to the illness within a couple of months. The severest punishment in jail was solitary confinement. The prisoner was confined twenty-four hours and taken only to the bathroom. It was tormenting even to spend seven days in this condition and after six months even the strongest of them broke down. Confinement in a cage was still worse. These cages were very small, hardly sufficient for a prisoner to lie down. He had to eat, answer the call of nature there and also sleep there. Many prisoners were confined in such cages twenty-four hours. Master Chattar Singh, Amar Singh,

Jawala Singh and Lai Singh were confined in such cages each for years.

The medical facilities provided were severely inadequate. Common ailments like headache and stomachache were reprobated as 'feigning' problems. Political inmates with high temperature were treated while still-locked in their cells. Barry never permitted the admission of a political prisoner in the jail hospital without his consent. Barry rather used to threaten the doctor that since he was a Hindu, he should not believe these prisoners and only those persons be considered sick who were so declared by him (Barry). The political prisoner was not admitted to the hospital till he was actually confined to bed and the doctor declared the prisoner as sick only when he was on his deathbed. If the matter was brought to the notice of higher authorities, Barry used to label these complaints as 'false allegations' and the chief commissioner believed him and in turn threatened the prisoners with dire punishment if such false allegations were repeated. Nobody in the jail was concerned with the fate of the political prisoners.

Conditions on Ship Board

Transported convicts were handed over to the master of a ship at the beginning of the voyage and formally transferred into the custody of the Governor of the colony who was receiving them. Indents, or indentures, were the documents used to record the transaction on arrival. Convicts were housed below decks on the prison deck and often further confined behind bars. In many cases they were restrained in chains and were only allowed on deck for fresh air and exercise. Conditions were cramped and they slept on hammocks. Very little information seems to be available about the layout of the convict ships, which ply between Calcutta and Andaman. Cruel masters, harsh discipline and scurvy, dysentery and typhoid resulted in a huge loss of life during journey. Usually the ship took a week or some times it may take at least ten days to reach Andamans. The convicts were lying in block and everyone was suffering from sea-sickness. For many convicts it was first sea voyage and worsened during monsoon. The police that escorted were mostly people of the Pathans. Some of them stood guard over day and night. At night sleep was not possible. The prisoner's blocks were big iron cages just of the type in which at times animals were carried on railway wagons. These were round the boilers of the ship-quite dark even during the day time. Dim lights were burning there the whole time. The atmosphere was suffocating. Convicts stand for hours together breathing in the freshness of the vast open sea. By the time the exiles were being transported in the 1860s and onwards, a more enlightened routine was in place which even included the presence on board of a Religious Instructor to educate the convicts and attend to their spiritual needs.

Similar experience was also mentioned by Bejoy Kumar Sinha, an Ex-Lahore Conspiracy case prisoner who was deported to Andaman Jail. He was sent to Andaman in 1932 right from Rajahmandri Jail, Andhra Pradesh. The ship which he embarked named 'Maharajah', the government charted boat that was to carry the comrades to Andaman along with other prisoners. They were kept in dark cellars in the bottom of the ship and were locked up. There were also large number of ordinary prisoners who were going to the islands but they were kept separated from them and all huddled together like so many cattle. Ship engines roared and the ship sailed to its voyage. There was a big hole –like opening for ventilation in each block. Their departure from motherland was very painful.

The prison life in Cellular Jail was rightly remarked as 'Hellish Inferino', which means a deadly jail was not less than a hell on earth. Much has been heard about the Devil Island, but the Cellular Jail was not less than the life of Devil Island. For a small lapse the Jail authorities execute brutal assaults on political prisoners. The political prisoners were kept in worst conditions and executed a most vindictive treatment.

Convicts were housed below decks on the prison deck and often further confined behind bars. In many cases they were restrained in chains and were only allowed on deck for fresh air and exercise. Conditions were cramped and they slept on hammocks. Very little information seems to be available about the layout of the convict ships, but a few books do contain artists' impressions and reproductions of images held in library collections. Although the convicts of the first fleet arrived in relatively good condition, the same cannot be said for those that followed during the rest of the century. Cruel masters, harsh discipline and scurvy, dysentery and typhoid resulted in a huge loss of life.

Many prisoners experienced the most difficult journey in the clogged bunk of the ship, the prisoners in chains could behold the Cellular Jail from the ship anchored about two to three miles away from Port Blair. From the ship they were taken to the shores of the Andamans. Then the revolutionaries in fetters were led to the Jail on foot with beds over their heads and utensils in hand. The enormous iron gates devoured them as it were and after crossing the corridor, they were taken in the open courtyard from where the inner structure presented a close eerie appearance. The convicts were provided the jail uniform consisting of shorts, a shirt measuring a little below the waist and a white cap. The sacred thread of the Hindus was removed, contrary to the practice in Indian jails. The political prisoners were shut up in small grimy cells during the night. In the room was kept a low bedstead hardly wide enough to allow comfortable sleep. One was to be most vigilant as a least careless turn could land the sleeper with a bang on the floor.

There was no urinal or lavatory near the cells for emergency use at night. Only an earthen pot painted with tar was kept in a corner of the cell, which was brought by the sweeper regularly every afternoon just before the prison was closed and he used to take it away in the morning. But it was very difficult to answer the call of nature in this pot. This was the most painful experience for the political inmates. If one by some means eased himself in the pot, it created the problem of bad odour. In the morning the prisoner had to request the sweeper to clean it and if the latter did not agree, he himself had to do it. It was considered to be a wrongdoing and the inmate was punished with handcuffs and standing handcuffs.

A loin cloth was given to each of the political prisoners for wearing while having a bath. It was so thin that it could hardly conceal any part of the body. Thus, when they had to change clothes, they were in a total helpless condition. They only had to submit to their fate; the inmates hung their head in shame. Wholesome food could not be expected in such a situation. A dabbu, (the broken half of the coconut shell) full of Kanji, the salt less and tasteless gruel of rice churned in water, dal and little vegetable were dispensed to the inmates. On occasion, even kerosene oil was mixed in the Kanji. The daily ration as per rules consisted of rice 6 oz., flour for roti 5 oz., dal 2 oz., salt 1 gram, oil one gram and vegetable 8 oz. for every prisoner irrespective of their needs. Even this quantity of daily food did not reach the prisoners in this jail, as they had to part with their quota of wheat chapattis and give them to the Muslim prisoners turned warders and remain content with rice gruel under the threat that they would be punished on fake charges. Curd, which was given to the prisoners only once a week, was always snatched by the petty officers and the jamadars. The inmates' appalling conditions were even more intensified with the cooks and caterers in the jail being more intimidating and a few of them stricken with diseases. Their dirty clothes, their perspiring bodies, the perspiration dripping down into the big pots of curry and rice which they brought out to serve, were all open to the view of the political prisoners. The kacha and un-skinned green plantain, roots, stalks and leaves boiled together with sand gravel and excretions of mice were served to the prisoners. They had to devour such "dainty" dishes with hungry glee, in the dirty iron dishes, which could not be cleaned even after great effort. The prisoners had to be seated in a line while eating, irrespective of the weather. If somebody moved away from the line to seek shelter, he was abused and punished. Besides, the petty officers never gave them sufficient time to finish their meals. They had to stop and get up when the signal 'the time is up' was raised by the jamadars. After the hard manual toil one needed water for washing and drinking. Even the water, the prime necessity of life was scarce in quantity for political prisoners. The luxury of having a bath was unthinkable. Only three katoras (shallow dish) of saltish sea-water was given for bathing. Sea-water was given not only for bathing and washing clothes but also for all other purposes except for drinking. The inmates were even denied reading material. Only one book was given to each of them on a Sunday morning in the first week and in the evening it used to be collected back. The exchange of books with the other prisoners was prohibited and breaking the code invited standing handcuffs for several days. No paper, slate or pencil was allowed to the prisoners.

Resistance in Cellular Jail

The revolutionary prisoners had brought about a pioneering change in the course of life for the British. Much as they wished to subdue the patriots, the undeterred heroes did fear for none. And with enlightened leaders, educated and level-headed to the limit that they could gauge every cunning move of the British, things at times turned worse for the ruling autocrats. They tried to enchain them in the hideous Cellular Jail, just to isolate them from the society and make a mockery of their daily life and radical activities. These revolutionaries were thus convicted for political offence, and Lord Minto, the governor-general of India, in his letter to the provincial governments had referred to these prisoners as 'political prisoners'. But they were never treated so and were denied the privileges as permissible to the political prisoners, as is evident from the government letter of 2nd August 1910, by which the chief commissioner, Andamans was directed not to call them political prisoners as it would 'tend to give them a spurious importance'. In turn, the commissioner in his letter of 9th September 1910 ensured its observance.

David Barry, head overseer and jailor of the Cellular, took the precaution not to call them 'political prisoners', nor did he tolerate the use of this expression by any of his subordinates. "There is none here of that kind", he used to say and he termed them disdainfully as the 'despicable lot', 'vagrant wretches' and 'scum of the society'. They were treated as 'dangerous prisoners' and a badge with the letter 'D' used to hang round the neck of political prisoners.

The revolutionaries spent a gruesome and agonising life in the Cellular Jail until they were released. The memoirs of Barindra Kumar Ghose, titled *The Tale of My Exile* (1922), Upendra Nath Bandyopadhyaya's *Nirvasiter Atmakatha* (Bengali) and Vinayak Damodar Savarkar's *Mqjhi Janmathep* (Marathi) along with its English translation *The Story of my Transportation for Life* (1950) by Prof. VN. Naik and the Hindi translation *Aajanm Karavas* (1966), portray in detail the excruciating routine, which the prisoners underwent in this godforsaken place. All of them spent almost ten years in this jail during 1909 to 1921 and their narration concerns this period. Ullaskar Dutt who left the Andamans in 1913 also penned down his memoirs. Some other revolutionaries who were gaoled in this jail from 1915-21 have also written about their experiences.

Administering physical and mental torture to the political prisoners was the premeditated plan of the British, with the idea that such severe punishment would keep them in check. However, they misapprehended the magnitude of the national spirit. These revolutionary patriots were built up quite in a different mould. Even after a year, authorities did not change their atrocious behaviour towards them. The year was 1911. The voice of resistance was first raised by a Punjabi prisoner, Nand Gopal, sentenced to expatriation for ten years for writing 'seditious' articles in his Urdu weekly *Swaraj*, Allahabad, which he edited. He staged non-violent resistance against working on the oil mill. Nand Gopal's silent, yet defiant attitude shook David Barry, the dreaded jailor, and for perhaps for the very first time he felt humiliated and left the place in a huff. The erosion and nervousness of the authority was witnessed in a new light. This extraordinary incident filled the political prisoners with resilience: Nand Gopal was punished. He was given a reduced diet, but it did not deter him. He was determined to resist the inhuman treatment meted out by the jail authorities. The resistance displayed by Nand Gopal adversely affected the 'discipline' of the jail. But after a few days, he was again assigned work at the *kohlu*. He challenged the authorities that he would not do the *kohlu* work as he was a human being and not a bullock. It was an open defiance. Nand Gopal was put in chains and fetters. He was given a reduced diet and was confined. Also, a general order was issued that everybody would have to work on the oil-mill for three days. This created a stir and instigated a combative urge in the other prisoners to fight for their rights. They refused to work on the mill. Thus the strike began. Rigorous measures were adopted by the authorities to punish the strikers. Karyi, powdered rice in water, which could not be given for more than four days was served to all the strikers, but Ullaskar, Nand Gopal and Hoti Lal were fed on this abominable gruel for two weeks continuously. The strikers were handcuffed. Several forms of punishment were inflicted on them one after the other. They were kept in solitary confinement and were not allowed to communicate with each other. But they did not veer off. They held out against all odds. The authorities gave in and assured them work outside the jail with no work on the oil mills. It was the first major victory of the political prisoners in the whole epic resistance. The patriots stood united like a rock and succeeded in defeating plans of the British, although it was at the price of numerous penalties and physical sufferings. V.D. Savarkar was also brought to the Andaman about this time to undergo his fifty years' sentence.

His fellow captives included many political prisoners, who were forced to perform hard labour for many years. Reunited with his brother Ganesh, the Savarkars nevertheless struggled in the harsh environment. It included waking up and performing at 5 a.m., tasks including cutting trees and chopping wood, and working at the oil mill under regimental strictness, with talking amidst prisoners strictly prohibited during mealtime. Prisoners were subjects to frequent mistreatment and torture. Contact with the outside world and home was restricted to the writing and mailing of one letter a year. In these years, Savarkar withdrew within himself and performed his routine tasks mechanically. Obtaining permission to start a rudimentary jail library, Savarkar would also teach some fellow convicts to read and write.

> 'I hereby acknowledge that I had a fair trial and just sentence. I heartily abhor methods of violence resorted to in days gone by and I feel myself duty bound to uphold law and constitution to the best of my powers and I am willing to make the Reform [1919 Montague-Chelmsford Reforms] a success in so far as I may be allowed to do so in future'

Savarkar appealed for clemency in 1911 and again during Sir Reginald Craddock's visit in 1913, citing poor health in the oppressive conditions. In 1920, the Indian National Congress and leaders such as Mahatma Gandhi, Vithalbhai Patel and Bal Gangadhar Tilak demanded his unconditional release. Savarkar tactically signed a statement endorsing the trial, verdict and British law, and renouncing violence, a bargain for freedom. Savarkar appealed for clemency within a year of his reaching the Andamans. In one of his communications, he says,

> '...if the government in their manifold beneficence and mercy release me, I for one cannot but be the staunchest advocate of constitutional progress and loyalty to the English government which is the foremost condition of that progress ... Moreover, my conversion to the constitutional line would bring back all those misled young men in India and abroad who were once looking up to me as their guide.'

On May 2, 1921, the Savarkar brothers were moved to a jail in Ratnagiri, and later to the Yeravda Central Jail. He was finally released on January 6, 1924 under stringent restrictions – he was not to leave Ratnagiri District and was to refrain from political activities for the next five years. However, police restrictions on his activities would not be dropped until provincial autonomy was granted in 1937.

The second spectacular victory for these strong-willed revolutionaries was their success in informing their countrymen about the nightmarish conditions in the Andaman jail where they were lodged and the cruel treatment meted out to them. The prisoners frustrated the British plans of withholding from the world all information regarding the cellular administration of political prisoners. Hoti Lal of Haryana, editor of *Swaraj*, undergoing his sentence in the Cellular Jail and listed as 'incorrigible', wrote a three page letter covering all the aspects of distressing life of the political prisoners in the jail. He signed the letter mentioning the number of his cell. He took an ordinary prisoner in confidence, gave him the letter and ensured that it reached Surendranath Banerjee, the renowned nationalist and editor of *Bengalee* in Calcutta. The plan was successful and Surendranath published the full account of the horrible life of political prisoners in the Andamans on 4, 8 and 20 September 1911 in his paper. Among other things, the articles exposed the authorities for, (i) giving inedible diet on the slightest pretext, (ii) forcing the prisoners to work in jungles involving hard labour, (iii) forcing them to work in spite of ill-health and (iv) consequential loss of weight by many of them who were virtually reduced to skeletons. The convicts learnt of the whole affair only when one day Barry holding a stick in his hands, in full fury stood near Hoti Lal Verma's cell and fiercely reprimanded the warders in expletive terms. He abused the prisoners and also asked Hoti Lal to stand up and called him a 'liar'. The other political prisoners were aghast at his behaviour but Hoti Lal could clearly make out that his plan had succeeded. When the others learnt of this, they were wonderstruck. This stirred the Indians and the British authorities had to act with their backs to the wall to defend them. By this time Nani Gopal of Chinsura, Pulin Behari Das of Dacca and some other patriots had also arrived in the Cellular Jail.

The next resistance was the second general and hunger strike by some of them, leading to the acceptance of their demands. The suicide by Indubhusan Roy and Ullaskar's insanity led to the second general strike. The political prisoners prepared a charter of demands which included - (i) proper food, (ii) release from hard labour, and (iii) freedom to associate with each other. It was sent to the authorities. Since the prisoners were aware that the authorities would not yield to any of the demands, therefore, the next course of action was also already planned by them. The plan of general strike was brought into action. A few political prisoners joined in the beginning but the others continued joining it, day by day. The political prisoners were nonetheless, a determined lot. They refused to stand up as a mark of respect on the arrival of Barry. They violated the jail rules by talking to each other loudly so as to be audible to the co-prisoners, who were locked in cells at a distance. The abusive language used by the jail officials was replied by more forceful language. When the warders assaulted one or two of them, the political prisoners cautioned them with dire consequences. During the general strike, although none of the political prisoners conceded to the penalties and pressures of the jail authorities, Noni Gopal, a young man, proved to be the toughest fighter in the wake of pressures and blatant physical torture.

The news about Indubhusan's suicide, Ullaskar's insanity and Noni Gopal's hunger strike reached the country. The press started a vigorous campaign. The government was compelled to send Dr. (Percy) Lukis, director of the Indian Medical Services to make an inquiry. But his report was not published, although as a consequence, Ullaskar was sent over to the asylum in Madras and the others also heaved a sigh of relief for some time at least. Nani Gopal, after considerable difficulty, was also persuaded by his friends to eat. A little after this, the prisoners from outside were sent out again as their term expired. Noni Gopal was on a hunger strike for seventy-two days and the strike came to an end on 6th December 1912. In this long-drawn struggle, the political prisoners were able to get some concessions. They got the permission of the jail superintendent to get books into the prison. They got the complete works of Herbert Spenser, Shakespeare, Mill, Swami Vivekananda, Ramakrishna, Gibbon, Emerson, Macaulay and the famous books like *Republic* by Plato, Utopia by Sir Thomas Moore, and works of well-known Maratha and Bengali poets. At the time of Savarkar's departure, there were 2000 books in the jail library. *Satyarth Parkash* in Hindi by Swami Dayanand Saraswati was read by many. The jail authorities even permitted the political prisoners to sit together, read books or hold discussions, but their duties continued and they were asked not to resort to strikes or agitations.

The British authorities were highly aware of the capabilities of the political prisoners and were so apprehensive of their activities that they were alarmed at the information given to them in August 1913 by one Lal Mohan, a Bengali prisoner that a bomb factory was started in the island by the political prisoners working in the settlement. Rumours were set afloat that a bomb was found in an adjoining brook; that there was a plan for destroying the whole settlement of Port Blair and engaging the boats to take the prisoners across the sea. The authorities became alert. Searches were made at all possible places of slight suspicion. A special police officer was called from Calcutta to investigate. Explosive experts also reached the Andamans. The political prisoners working outside were locked in their cells. They were not too happy with their freedom being curtailed and they made representations to the Government of India that either they be prosecuted on the charges against them, or they be sent outside for work.

Lieutenant Colonel Douglas was the superintendent in Port Blair during that time. After the rumours of the alleged conspiracy of bomb making, two successive strikes of the political prisoners, publication of letters from them in newspapers, newspaper reports about their dreadful adversities and agonies, subsequent public agitation and questions asked in the Imperial Legislative Council, and lastly, the suspected conspiracy to prepare bombs, at last convinced the Government of India that there was something very nasty going on in the settlement at Port Blair. So an official of high rank, the Home Member of the Governor General's Council, Sir Reginald Craddock, visited the Andamans in October 1913 to see things for himself. Although his visit was kept secret from the political prisoners, they still learnt about it. Birendra Chandra Sen, Upendra Nath Banerjee, Nand Gopal, Hoti Lal Verma and Pulin Behari Das appeared before him and without caring for the resulting punishments, they openly impeached the jail authorities regarding the deprivation of their rights. Y.D. Savarkar had detailed discussion with Craddock. Y.D. Savarkar, Hrishi Kesh Kanjilal, Barindra Kumar Ghose, Nand Gopal and Sudhir Kumar Sarkar, each of them also handed over petitions to him for the government's consideration. These were noticed and discussed by the Home member in his report dated 23rd November 1913, written by him on board S.S. Maharaja on the return journey. These petitions were also appended with the report, which contained first-hand information of the political prisoners about their life in the Cellular Jail. The prisoners again decided to fight when even after Craddock's visit things did not alter in their favour.

This, however, did not daunt the political prisoners to fight for their due recognition. Hrishikesh Kanjilal and G.D. Savarkar wrote to the Government of India for treating them as political prisoners, but the government in November 1912 informed the superintendent of the jail that "the prisoners should be given clearly to understand that they were not to be considered as political prisoners". Noni Gopal Mukherjee continued a grim battle to get it conceded from the government. Some of the other independent, educated activists included Maulana Fazl-e-Haq Khairabadi, Maulana Ahmadullah, Maulvi Abdul Rahim Sadiqpuri, Vinayak Damodar Savarkar, Ganesh Savarkar, Bhai Parmanand, Sohan Singh, Vaman Rao Joshi, Nand Gopal, Ullaskar Dutt, Indubhusan Roy, Barindra Kumar Ghosh and Dr. Diwan Singh Kalepani.

Although according to the government's instructions, the political prisoners were to be considered as ordinary prisoners, they were actually treated worse than ordinary prisoners from every angle. These educated prisoners were assigned tough manual jobs, whereas ordinary prisoners with meager knowledge of even the English alphabet were given the light work in the printing press or the work of a munshi (clerk). The ordinary convicts deployed on hard labour were released and promoted as warders and petty officials, which was not in the lot of political prisoners. Any ordinary convict below twenty years of age was not employed on the oil-mill, but a political prisoner of any age was so employed indiscriminately. The political inmates were treated differently even in the jail hospital. An ordinary convict was provided medical attention unlike political prisoners.

They had to walk a distance of five to ten miles, shivering all the while with fever and carrying beds and utensils over their shoulders. Ordinary convicts had the liberty to speak to each other, which was denied to the political prisoners. Ordinary convicts were released from the Cellular Jail after a period of six months and were sent outside for work. But the political prisoners were kept inside the Jail for years at a stretch. The privilege of earning remission was not allowed to them. They could never hope to become self-supporting convicts. As life within the jail was quite macabre and unbearable, the political prisoners voiced their desire to work outside, because of comparative diverse facilities. The work was light and the food was better. There was freedom of company and speech. The admission in the hospital outside was much easier compared to the jail hospital. The political inmates fought for it and after the first general strike in the Cellular Jail, some of the political prisoners were sent outside to work. The working outside too became a suffering, as they were at work from 6 to 10 in the morning and 1 to 4.30 in the afternoon. They were harshly exposed to rain and the scorching sun. The workers in the forests faced several other hardships. Their ration was stolen and sold in the villages and medical facilities were denied to them. The outside work proved a delusion and one by one they came back to the dungeon cells to be consumed inside the jail. The political prisoners were not allowed to communicate with each other. All conversation was illegal and vocative of the "Barry principle" of administration. The stern Pathan-jamadar Khoyedad used to keep a check on the interaction between the prisoners. The only opportunity for them to inquire about the health of the co-accused by signal was at a common place, i.e., during the time of bathing at the tank or at mealtimes, but if any of them was found talking; he was punished with seven days standing handcuffs. The warder was transferred to another section if by civility he conveyed the good wishes of one prisoner to the other. Talking to the authorities about a co-prisoner was also considered an offence.

Japanese atrocities

Japanese behaviour initially was cordial and most of the islanders thought that the bad days were over. Immediately after the occupation, the Japanese released all convicts from the gaol cells where the most dangerous characters were confined. Thereafter, convicts, local-born inhabitants and free settlers were permitted to move freely except in certain prohibited areas, such as the aerodrome and naval dockyard. This soon changed and many gruesome atrocities took place. Some nationalist Indians sympathized with the Japanese as the alleged liberators from the British joke. They were soon to be disillusioned. Looting, wrecking, atrocities on local population, the setting free of dangerous criminals, and forced labour from dawn to dusk at slave wages form the first news from Port Blair, in the Andaman Islands, since the occupation by the Japanese on Andaman island. During the first week of occupation, the Japanese freely looted homes and business places, wildly wrecked private and public property and committed their now notorious characteristic atrocities on women and children. While all this was in progress, the Japanese authorities set up a system of forced labour, under which the local inhabitants were made to do coolie work from dawn to dusk at the equivalent of a shilling a day.

The early days of the Japanese occupation of Andaman Islands brought unexpected sorrows and intimidation on local intellectuals (mostly officials and doctors). They were encouraged to join Rash Behari Bose's Indian Independence League, and a 'Peace Committee' was formed from its members, headed by Dr. Diwan Singh. Over the next few months they did what they could to mitigate the suffering of the population at the hands of the Japanese, but to little avail: indeed, many of them would later fall victim themselves. Forced labour was used to build a new airport, and in October 1942 mass arrests of 'spies' took place, with 300 people being confined in the Cellular Jail, where some were tortured. Of these seven were shot, including Narayan Rao, who had been Superintendent of Police under Japanese auspices, Itter Singh, the Deputy Superintendent, Subedar Sube Singh of the Military Police and Dr. Surinder Nag.

Realising that the Japanese were targeting influential members of the population, the members of the Indian Independence League grew increasingly nervous, and ceased to engage in much nationalist activity. In 1943 a second reign of terror was unleashed by the new commander of the garrison, Colonel Jochi Renusakai and Chief of Police Mitsubashi, both of whom had served at Nanking. Six hundred people were arrested and tortured, including Dr. Diwan Singh, who died as a result of injuries.

Reign of Terror

In the first week of June, 1945, hundreds of educated families were lodged in the cellular jail on a false promise that they were to be taken to a virgin soil to lead a comfortable life. They were boarded on a number of transport aircrafts. On sighting the Havelock Island, situated at a distance of 50 miles from Port Blair, they were ordered to jump in the sea. Whoever hesitated was beaten with rifle butts while others were struck with swords and bayonets. Out of 1500, about 250 swam ashore only to die of hunger and starvation. In a fortnight half of them died; the rest were struggling to survive on the leaves and barks of trees, as the soil was saline and unproductive. In the end only one person by the name of Mohammad Saudagar survived to tell their story of woe. Within a week of this cold-blooded massacre the Japanese chased about 900 people from several villages and gathered them in a central village to 'facilitate their transportation' to a nearby island. After keeping them hungry for 24 hours they were taken to Tarmugli Island where they were all tied to trees and used for bayonet practice. Petrol was sprinkled over them and the dead were burned to ashes along with some who were burned alive.

More than 2000 people were crammed in the Cellular Jail and due to the shortage of space the remaining few hundred were kept in Thokuman and Namtal. They were starved and beaten, and a large number of them died. Apart from these massacres, hundreds of people were killed in villages and on roads. The whole island had become an inferno. Out of the total population of 40,000 in Port Blair, 30,000 were annihilated. This holocaust is unknown to the world, maybe because it was a penal settlement for dreaded convicts and freedom fighters. The world along with Japan grieves every year for the victims of the atom bomb. But historians and journalists have not made any effort to mark the mass killings of innocent people at Port Blair, complete devastation of Andaman island, continuous suffering of the people for a period of three-and-a-half years. Meanwhile Japanese politicians and bureaucrats have made deliberate efforts to distort or cover up the facts of history.

The first victim of the Japanese occupation of Andaman Islands came on the fourth day after their landing. Angered by soldiers who had pursued some chickens into his house, a young man called Zulfiqar Ali fired an airgun at them. No-one was hurt, but he was forced into hiding. After twenty-four hours he was captured and marched to the *maidan* in front of the Browning Club. Here his arms were twisted until they broke, and he was then shot. A cement memorial now stands on the spot. A trial of a British officer Major A.G. Bird, who had not been sent to Rangoon or Singapore like the other British captives, and of whom the Japanese were determined to make an example. Pushkar Bakshi persuaded a fellow convict, Sarup Ram, to bear witness at Bird's 'trial' that he had been spying (wireless parts had been planted in the house where he was imprisoned). It has been suggested that Bakshi had a grudge against Bird for having given him a six-month sentence for theft before the Japanese invasion. According to eyewitnesses Bird, a popular man known as "Chirrie" ('Bird' in Hindi) had his arms and legs twisted and broken, and was then beheaded by Colonel Bucho with his sword. At this stage the Japanese decided that Bakshi was no longer useful, and he was imprisoned.

The ghastly torture of Dr. Diwan Singh, whose spirits the dark times failed to paralyse and who set aside all precautions in resisting the unpredictable Japanese. This gruesome event of Japanese Barbarism must be added to those already infamous stories known around the world about the savagery waged by the Japanese. The boundaries of Japanese misdeeds are wide and scattered. Diwan Singh was brutally tortured for 82 days along with other companions, a parallel of which is difficult to find in history. He was hung by his hair from the ceiling. Alternately, his ankles were tied to the ceiling while water was pumped through his mouth and nostrils, he was tied to a stake as his bones were crushed and electric shocks were given. Unbelievably, fires was lit under his thighs; nails pulled from his fingers and toes. Strips of flesh were peeled from various parts of his body daily. He was even forced to sit on a charcoal stove. Though they ended his torture by gouging out his eyes the Japanese were never able to break the Doctor's spirit. He died on January 14, 1944.

Meanwhile, local women were being 'recruited' by Bagchi to act as "comfort women" for the Japanese garrison. Their discontent subsequently Korean and Malay women being brought in instead. Forced labour was used to build a new airport, and in October 1942 mass arrests of 'spies' took place, with 300 people being confined in the Cellular Jail, where some were tortured. Of these seven were shot, including Narayan Rao, who had been Superintendent of Police under Japanese auspices, Itter Singh, the Deputy Superintendent, Subedar Sube Singh of the Military Police and Dr. Surinder Nag. Realising that the Japanese were targeted influential members of the population, the members of the Indian Independence League grew increasingly nervous, and ceased to engage in much nationalist activity. In 1943 a second reign of terror was unleashed by the new commander of the garrison, Colonel Jochi Renusakai, and Chief of Police Mitsubashi, both of whom had served at Nanking. Six hundred people were arrested and tortured, including Dr. Diwan Singh, who died as a result of grievious injuries. At this stage the Japanese decided that Bagchi was no longer useful, and he was imprisoned.

The Arzi Hukumat-e-Azad Hind

On December 29, 1943, political control of the islands was theoretically passed to the Azad Hind government of Subhas Chandra Bose. Bose visited Port Blair to raise the tricolor flag of the Indian National Army. During his visit to the Andamans, he was kept carefully screened from the local population by the Japanese authorities. Various attempts were made to inform him of the sufferings of the people of the Andamans, and the fact that many local Indian Nationalists were at that time being tortured in the Cellular Jail. Bose does not seem to have been aware of this, and the judgment of some is that he "failed his people". After Bose's departure, the Japanese remained in effective control of the Andamans, and the sovereignty of the *Arzi Hukumat-e Hind* was largely fictional. The islands themselves were renamed "Shaheed" and "Swaraj", meaning "martyr" and "self-rule" respectively. Bose appointed General Loganathan as the governor of the islands, and had limited involvement with the administration of the territory. During his interrogation after the war Loganathan admitted that he had only had full control over the islands' vestigial education department, as the Japanese had retained control over the police force, and in protest he had refused to accept responsibility for any other areas of Government. He was powerless to prevent the worst Japanese atrocity of the occupation, the 'Homfreyganj massacre' of the 30th January 1944, where forty-four Indian civilians were shot by the Japanese on suspicion of spying. Many of them were members of the Indian Independence League. Notionally this government continued to administer the islands, which were almost the only territory it ever acquired, until the British retook them in 1945, but in practice little had changed. Casualties on the more sparsely-populated Nicobar Islands were fewer, as the Japanese did not have a garrison there, although in 1943 they created a brief reign of terror on Car Nicobar as they rounded up forced labour amongst the Nicobarese. Subhas Chandra Bose set up his "independent India" at Port Blair and unrolled there what some Indian nationalists still regard as a turning point in Indian history, the "first flag of an independent India". The occupation left a legacy of lasting bitterness towards the Japanese, and to some extent towards their collaborators in the *Arzi-Hukumat-e Azad Hind,* amongst the generation which experienced it.

REFERENCES

1. Brown, Giles (August 1948). The Hindu Conspiracy, 1914-1917. *The Pacific Historical Review.* University of California Press.
2. Collins, Larry; Lapierre, Dominique (1997). *Freedom at Midnight.* London: Harper Collins.
3. Chandra, Bipan; Mridula Mukherjee, Aditya Mukherjee, Sucheta Mahajan, K.N. Panikkar (1989). *India's Struggle for Independence.* New Delhi: Penguin Books.
4. Dasgupta. Jayant, (2002) Japanese in Andaman & Nicobar Islands. *Red Sun over Black Water,* Delhi, Manas Publications.
5. Heehs, Peter (1998). *India's Freedom Struggle: A Short History.* Delhi: Oxford University Press
6. Fraser, Thomas G (1977). Germany and Indian Revolution, 1914-18. *Journal of Contemporary History, Vol. 12, No. 2* (April, 1977), Sage Publications.
7. Hoover, Karl. (May 1985). The Hindu Conspiracy in California, 1913-1918. *German Studies Review,* German Studies Association.
8. Forest, G.W. (2000). *The Indian Mutiny 1857-1858.* Delhi: Low Price Publications.
9. Hopkirk, Peter (1997). *Like Hidden Fire: The Plot to Bring Down the British Empire,* Kodansha Globe.
10. Lovett, Sir Verney (1920). *A History of the Indian Nationalist Movement.* New York, Frederick A. Stokes Company.
11. Mathur, L.P. (1985) *Kala Pani: History of the Andaman & Nicobar Islands with a study of India's Freedom Struggle,* Delhi: Eastern Book Corporation.
12. Nehru, Jawaharlal (1989). *Discovery of India.* Delhi: Oxford University Press.
13. Popplewell, Richard J (1995). *Intelligence and Imperial Defence: British Intelligence and the Defence of the Indian Empire 1904-1924..* Routledge.

14. Sarkar, Sumit (1983). *Modern India: 1885-1947.* Madras: Macmillan.
15. Sarkar, B.K. (March 1921). *Political Science Quarterly.* The Academy of Political Science.
16. Singh. N. Iqbal, (1978) *The Andaman Story,* Delhi, Vikas Publications.
17. Tinker, Hugh (October 1968). India in the First World War and after, *Journal of Contemporary History, 1918-19: From War to Peace,* Sage Publications.

5
Contribution of Andaman Islands to Indian Freedom Struggle

The First War of Independence in India was marked by atrocities committed by both sides, and ultimately led to the British Empire to consider injecting harsh punishment to all those subjects, who have raised voice against the regime. The first war of Independence of 1857 was a major turning point in the consolidation of Andaman Islands. The British recaptured the islands in 1858 and gradually introduced the penal administration to facelift the island territory into a penal colony. The then British embarked upon a penal system to reform the socially unmanageable groups like hard core criminals, dacoits especially politically recruited nationalists. They cleared the jungles, created infrastructure like roads, jetties, schools, hospitals and other amenities including modern facilities to make the islands a compact and isolated society different to mainland traditional ones. In doing so the British also severely faced all such humiliations and hardships like our forefathers. The decades following the settlement were a period of growing political awareness, manifestation of public opinion and emergence of national spirit among the local born which was the most significant feature. They were mostly members of the convict families and successful free-settlers (Local-Born) provincial elites, engaged in organizing the religious festivals to induce cultural affinity within the communities residing in Port Blair city. In the beginning there was no well-defined ideology of the islanders and it commanded few of the resources essential to a socio-political organization. It functioned more as a debating society that met annually to express its loyalty to the British Raj. The inculcation of religious ideas and social pride was fundamental to the rise of a public opinion on islander hood.

The rediscovery of revolutionaries in Andaman Islands led to the rise of nationalism especially by the youth inspired by the deeds of Noni Gopal, Veer Savarkar, Bhagat Singh, Raj Kumar, Sukhdev and many more. In fact there was no direct interaction with the revolutionaries jailed in Andaman Islands. But there were few instances of the local born taking part in national movement raising slogans for national consolidation. By 1900, although the local born had emerged as an effective social organization, their achievement was undermined by their failure to attract attention of others. Islanders felt that their representation in the then government service was inadequate. The diversity among Islanders, however, made it possible to bring about uniform cultural and intellectual regeneration within the social milieu. The nationalistic sentiments among Islanders were not lesser than their counterparts at mainland India. Since they were placed in isolation and living under adverse conditions, the local born could not in an open protest. The acts of political prisoners deeply left impressive marks on the youth. In fact the local born resented the denial of freedom of expression for political prisoners, and the lack of any voice to discourage the British master for their inhuman treatment. For these reasons, the local born considered freedom as the natural and only solution. Despite these atrocities the freedom fighters used to resist and fight for their self-respect and for the love of their country. Sher Ali was given life imprisonment during the Wahabi movement against the British Raj. He assassinated Lord Mayo, Viceroy of India with a knife on 8th February, 1872. He was hanged on Viper Island. This act of Sher Ali was acknowledged, justified and hailed as a patriotic act among the local Muslim brethren.

The Revolutionary Movement was prominent in Punjab through the Heroes of The Gadar party, The Hindustan Republican Association was in U.P. formed by Sachin Sanyal, in Maharashtra with the Savarkar brothers and of course with the partition of Bengal in 1905, secret societies and lots of underground groups were beginning to form. Lots of conspiracy cases started in the courts and the number of revolutionary freedom fighters in the jails began to swell. Most of the leaders of these movements if not hanged outright were deported to the Andaman Cellular Jail. Several died due to inhuman treatment and torture. This aroused the sentiments among the islanders and gained enough sympathy towards the cause of independence. In spite of all such incidents Andaman Islands contributed largely to the British World War I effort by providing men and resources. A good number of soldiers from Andaman Islands fought war in Europe, Africa, and the Middle East, and many lost their life while supplying food, money, and ammunition. To mark respect to those soldiers, the clock tower was erected in the post-World War I.

Nationalism in Andaman was closely linked with the unrests in Punjab, Bengal and elsewhere and was significant enough to nearly paralyse the penal administration. Also from the beginning of the war, the Gadar Party and Singapore mutiny remain most notable. This movement was suppressed by means of a massive internal counter-intelligence operation and draconian political acts (including the Defence of India Act 1915) that lasted nearly ten years. The pre-war nationalist movement revived as the moderate and extremist groups within the Congress submerged their differences in order to stand as a unified front. In 1916, the Congress succeeded in forging the Lucknow Pact, a temporary alliance with the Muslim League over the issues of devolution of political power and the future of Islam in the region. All these changes were significantly witnessed in cellular jail.

The Gadar Party whose president was Baba Sohan Singh and the secretary was Lala Har Dayal was formed in America to get our country free from the British. In 1914, with arms and ammunition, Gadar Party members, travelling by the ship Kama Gata Maru arrived in Calcutta. They were arrested by the British. A large number of Gadar party activists were jailed in Andaman Islands. This was evident from the records available in Andaman. In fact the Cellular Jail played a central role in fostering political consciousness among the inmates. Hindustan Socialist Republican Association was formed under the leadership of Chandrasekhar Azad. Bhagat Singh and Batukeshwar Dutt threw a bomb inside the Central Legislative Assembly on 8 April 1929 protesting against the passage of the Public Safety Bill and the Trade Disputes Bill. Following the trial (Central Assembly Bomb Case), Bhagat Singh, Sukhdev and Rajguru were hanged in 1931. Allama Mashriqi founded Khaksar Tehreek in order to direct particularly the Muslims towards the independence movement. Bhagat Singh's other friends Batukeshwar Dutt, Bejoy Kumar Sinha, Shiv Verma, Jaidev Kapoor, Dr. Gaya Prasad, Kamal Nath Tiwari, Mahabir Singh were given life imprisonment and were sent to Andaman Cellular Jail. These names are popular among the local born who respect them as freedom fighters.

The conditions became worst and the inmates of jail deprived of their basic needs. The food that was given was not fit for human consumption. Prisoners were not allowed to interact with other brethren. The warders carried out unbearable forms of physical torture and flogging. Their behaviour was insulting. Things had become unbearable. On 12 May 1933 the only alternative before the political prisoners was to resort to a hunger strike against these atrocities. Thus, they started a fast unto death. Mahavir Singh, Mohan Kishore Namo Das and Mohit Moitra died during the hunger strike. Their bodies were quietly ferreted away and thrown out to sea. Punjab's jail inspector, Barker was called to break the hunger strike. He issued orders to stop the issuing of drinking water. The freedom fighters were resolute. There was a huge outcry throughout India because of this hunger strike. After 46 days the British Raj had to bow and the demands of the freedom fighters had to be accepted. The hunger strike ended on 26 June 1933. After the death of three colleagues the facilities won from jail authorities proved beneficial for the future. Many more facilities including light in the cells, newspapers, books and periodicals were arranged for the benefit of inmates. The jail work was reduced to the minimal. Above all there was respect for the political prisoners from the prison officials and a marked improvement in their behaviour. A new environment was created in the jail and prisoners allowed to meet their colleagues to discuss and read issues pertaining to national movement. A Communist consolidation was formed of 39 prisoners on 26 April 1935. This number later swelled to 200. The freedom fighters started feeling that the atmosphere for a world war was gathering and that before the war started they should get back to their country to be with their people and take active part in the upheaval that was imminent. A petition was sent to the Viceroy on 9 July 1937 by the freedom fighters that all political prisoners should be repatriated to the mainland and released An ultimatum was given that if these demands were not met a hunger strike would begin.

A country wide movement on the mainland in support of the demands of the Andaman freedom fighters began as other political prisoners in other jails on the mainland also started hunger strikes in support. There was a mass demonstration of working people, intellectuals and students. This upsurge clearly showed that their people on the mainland did not forget them. After four weeks telegrams from Bengal's chief minister, leaders of the nation Jawaharlal Nehru, Subhash Chandra Bose, Sharad Chandra Bose, Rabindra Nath Tagore, etc, poured in imploring the freedom fighters to end their hunger strike.

On 28 August 1937, Gandhiji, poet Rabindra Nath Tagore and the Congress Working Committee sent a telegram..."the whole nation appeals to you to end the hunger strike... and assures you to take up your demands and to see them fulfilled..." After a lot of deliberation and discussion this historic 36-day hunger strike of 200 revolutionary freedom fighters ended. The process of repatriation started in September 1937. There were a total of 385 freedom fighters in jail at the time: 339 from Bengal, 19 from Bihar, 11 from Uttar Pradesh, 5 from Assam, 3 from Punjab, 2 from Delhi and 2 from Madras.

Meanwhile, the Island territory was occupied by Japanese forces. This event was a relief to political prisoners for their end of atrocities. Initially all the inmates of Cellular Jail were released. At mid-day on 29th December 1943, Netaji accompanied by Sarvashri Anand Mohan Sahay, Captain Rawat - ADC and Col. D.S. Raju, personal physician of Netaji, landed at the Port Blair aerodrome in the Andamans. He was received by the Japanese admiral at Port Blair. The enthusiastic Indians and Burmese also accorded a warm reception to him. Netaji went around the historic Cellular Jail where the walls told him, in silence, the woes of the political prisoners who were tortured there. He also saw the courage and enduring spirit that braved the vehemence of the British authorities. Netaji paid glowing tributes to the noble sacrifices of the Indian heroes. On the following day, 30th December 1943, the National Flag was hoisted by Netaji on the liberated Indian soil, an act, first of its kind in the history of the oppressive British rule in India. All the ceremonies of retrieving the lost territory from the enemy were held with joy, pride and jubilation. The national anthem i.e. the anthem of the Azad Hind Fauj (The Indian National Army) was sung in chorus by all present, which added to the gravity of the occasion. During the course of the day, the National Flag was hoisted at the Gymkhana Ground at Port Blair and atop the British Chief Commissioner's residence in the Ross Island, the then capital of the Islands. Netaji expressed the hope that some day soon the same flag would fly on the Viceroy's House in New Delhi. In a press interview in the first quarter of 1944, Netaji had stated that by the acquisition of the Andaman and Nicobar Islands, the provisional government had become a national entity, in fact, as well as in law. The liberation of the Andamans had symbolic significance, because the British always used them as a jail for political prisoners. Part by part, Indian territory would be liberated, but it was always the first plot of land that held the significance. The Andamans were renamed as 'Shaheed' in the memory of these martyrs and Nicobar as 'Swaraj'. Netaji's historic visit to the island made a symbolic fulfillment of his promise that INA would stand on the Indian soil by the end of 1943. The islanders celebrated the day with great enthusiasm and sensibility. The news of end of Second World War was generally welcomed by the local born. They were greatly excited over the prospects of overthrowing the foreign yoke and making India free.

To commemorate the memory of the freedom struggle and to inspire the future generations, the Ex-Andaman Freedom Fighters fraternity demanded the conversion of Cellular Jail into a National Memorial. On May 1969 the Government of India announced the three wings and the Central tower would be preserved as a national memorial. Shri. Vishwanath Mathur was instrumental in taking up the issue with the government in stopping the demolition of the wings of Cellular Jail and later raised the question in Parliament. This led to declaring it a National Memorial – the proud symbol of India's Revolutionary struggle for freedom. A decade later on February 11, 1979, the Cellular Jail was dedicated to the nation as a National Memorial by the then Prime Minister of India, Shri. Morarji Desai in a solemn ceremony in the midst of among others, scores of freedom fighters who were imprisoned in it as convicts. He said 'I want every Indian to be as strong and bold as those freedom fighters who had suffered in this Jail'. Although a symbol of gruesome holocaust as the colonial government wanted to make it, for the heroes of yester years it was a romantic reminiscence. They could not help being overpowered by emotions and nostalgia. Every visitor pays tribute to the memory of the freedom fighters by silently bowing before the memorial. It looks as if the voice of the martyrs, who sacrificed their lives for the cause, is vibrating through the corridors of the monument and asking the new generation which way they were moving?

The Andaman and Nicobar administration organized a solemn centenary function on 10th March 2006 to pay floral tributes to the heroes of Cellular Jail. The Ex-Andaman Political Prisoners and their family members also paid floral tributes to all the political prisoners. On this historic day a function was organized in the front of the Cellular Jail to felicitate all surviving Ex-Andaman Political Prisoners, spouses and close relatives of deceased freedom fighters. The three surviving political freedom fighters and 37 spouses of the freedom fighters who were present on the occasion added great spirit and inspiration for the younger generations. The three freedom fighters who were present on the occasion were Shri Bhowmick, Shri. Kartick Sarkar and Shri. Adhir Nag. The proud freedom fighters who assembled in front of Cellular Jail, recounted punishments given to them, ranging from extra hours on the grinding mill to standing handcuffed for a week, to bar-fetters for six months, to confinements in solitary cells, to four days of starvation diet and to cross bars for ten days a punishment which compelled the victim to keep his legs apart. Work on the oil-grinding mill was all the more terrible and caused several deaths. Often the prisoners became breathless, with their tongues parched up, limbs numb, hands bruised and the brain reeling. And their crime ? They loved their motherland.

The most touching moment which emotionally touched all was when the ashes of Shri. Vishwanath Mathur, a stalwart of Indian freedom movement, were immersed in the sea as per his last wish, the sea waters between the Cellular Jail and the Ross Island (the Headquarters of British empire) on March 11, 2006 raising the slogans *'Vishwanath Mathur amar rahe'* and *Ex-Andaman Political Prisoners amar rahe'* reverberated the air when Shri. Prakash Mathur, son of Vishwanath Mathur started poured the ashes into the sea.

About 30 spouses of freedom fighters along with Prakash Mathur with the ashes in the brass pot covered with garland and flowers started the journey for the immersion rituals from the gallery of the Cellular Jail, where Shri. Vishwanath Mathur was prisoned from 1934 to 1937. The boat 'Indu Bhusan' named after a freedom fighter took them all and after a fifteen minutes cruise, reached in an area between Cellular Jail and Ross Island pausing for conducting the immersion rituals. Patriotic songs and recitation of poems continued during the to and fro journey by the spouses of the freedom fighters on board the boat. Cellular Jail the Indian bastille of the pre-independence, now stands sanctified as the symbol of India's struggle for freedom. It is without doubt that the political prisoners in the Cellular Jail successfully passed the supreme test. They were not only prepared, but also eager to die for the cause. Inhuman physical and mental tortures failed to deter them from their firm resolve to free their motherland. In the dark solitary dungeons, hundreds of freedom fighters breathed their last for a glimpse of the dawn of freedom of their motherland. But when that moment came, the Cellular Jail stood forlorn and darksome. The Cellular Jail stands as a mute witness to the hallowed memory of those gallant revolutionaries, who made supreme sacrifices for the sake of their motherland. The saga of sacrifice, heroic deeds and the sufferings undergone by the valiant revolutionaries of India's freedom struggle will be remembered for ever and for generations to come.

Indeed the Andaman Islands are very closely connected with the saga of India's struggle for freedom and the movements of umpteen shades and types that shackled the British Empire in India. Once known for 'Kalapani' punishment now it has attained the name of 'Mukti Tirtha'. Indeed the Cellular jail was mute witness to the sufferings and sacrifices of political prisoners for the cause of their motherland. Every Indian should feel proud of those sons who have given up the prime of their youth. Away from their homes and hearth, away from the love and affection of their near and dear ones, undergone tremendous hardships, atrocities and humiliation in far off, inhospitable climate, their sole aim remained to free the motherland from foreign yoke.

However, the history has failed to do justice to the atrocities that occurred in the Andaman Islands during pre-independence. Details of the, all too human, slaughter of innocent, unarmed Indians at Port Blair may stimulate academicians and research scholars to make a fresh appraisal of the freedom movement of India. The oppressive and most undignified behaviour of the Japanese stunned the Indians who never expected such misconduct from the Japanese, who had popularized the slogan of a free South-east Asia. During the war, Japanese soldiers had executed many Islanders, mainly educated and intelligent local borns on suspicion that they were British spies. A record reveals in this regard that countless trials and mass executions took place, and hundreds of innocents, brought over from other islands on the pretext of rehabilitation, were pushed into the sea off Havelock Island. Many people are not aware of the Japanese brutalities particularly those of the Andaman and Nicobar Islands. It was a free for all. Men, women and children were shot dead or hacked by swords for no reason, the days of the wild Samurai, who had the power of life and death had returned—to the Andaman Island.

Today the entire islands became a symbol of sacrifice and courage and made a place in the hearts of every Indian for ever. Noni Gopal was one of those young revolutionaries and freedom fighters whose deeds of bravery and sacrifice have become the subject of discussion for many. He was one of those brave men who challenged the British rule in their own style. At the age of nineteen, he became a martyr, with "Vande Mataram" on his lips. Bhagat Singh became a legendary hero with masses. Innumerable songs were composed about him and the youth throughout the country made him their ideal. He became a symbol of bravery and a goal to free India. Long Live India And Long live it's peoples' memories are still kept alive in the youth of these islands. In fact we have failed to realise the dreams of our freedom fighters to build a strong and united nation. The silent majority watched in horror, whilst a great nation with an ancient civilisation, steeped in one of the finest cultural and architectural heritages of the world, nurtured in the traditions of the noble Buddhist philosophy of peace, tolerance and love veered off into a terrifying era of ethnic, political and social violence.

"Swadeshi Movement" in Bengal heralded a new age in our national history. Swadeshi was instantly identified as the highest form of patriotism and "Swadeshism" became the cradle of new India. It was an intensely spiritual movement and aimed at the emancipation of India in every sense, of all Indians. With fervent national calls for the boycott of British goods, schools, courts and administration gave stirring appeals for embracing "Swadeshi" in all spheres of life, indigenous manufactures, national education, language, literature and above all "Swaraj" or political freedom became the life breath of the nation.

The Swadeshi Movement was not just a political movement or an economic movement, it was a movement for total emancipation of every Indian in all walks of life political, economic, social, cultural and above all spiritual. The nation would not from the very beginning have raised the cry of "BANDE MATARAM" all the way in that context and in that connection and thrown itself into the "Swadeshi Movement" with such feverish energy, passion, impetuosity and vigorous enthusiasm had it not embraced all aspects of national life. "Bande Mataram" was on the lips of every revolutionary and every freedom fighter that was gaoled in Cellular jail. "Swadeshi", "British Boycott" and "Bande Mataram" all became vital, vigorous and vibrant interchangeable watchwords of all freedom fighters in Andaman Islands.

Andaman Islands have contributed significantly in the freedom struggle of the country. The initiative, bravery, guts and headship that the political prisoners have showed in the freedom movements for the country's independence from colonial rule have given them widespread significance in the Andaman society. During the hunger strikes, the local born indirectly supported the political prisoners to fulfill their ambition for an independent India. The local born actively participated in the revolution and movement for social change during the national struggle for independence. Thus, the participation of local born was not restricted to one type of activity such as the non-violent Satyagraha Movement. their early contribution to the national movement started in the late 19th Century with the involvement in the Indian National Congress.

During the freedom struggle of the country, local born were not lagging behind. They also joined the silent protest against the British rulers as and when atrocities reached sky limit. Many local born volunteered to give service to Indian National Army (INA), which was set up by Subhash Chandra Bose. This was one of the most genuine and fearless movements undertaken by Indian men and women under the able and remarkable leadership of this great patriot. Some unpublished records certify that on appeal from Netaji Subhash Chandra Bose, a large number of around 1000 men and women volunteered to support the cause of freedom movement. The real impact of the INA may not have been in military terms, but it had a deep psychological impact on the Andaman islanders. While there was significant number of men patriots who stood by Gandhiji and the Congress party in the struggle for independence. The local born took keen interest in the day to day progress of the freedom struggle of India and few excelled as speakers, marchers, campaigners and tireless volunteers. They also actively participated in the processions and rallies conducted by the local political parties. The contribution of Andaman Islands in freedom struggle of India is truly remarkable and is difficult to define in words. Their contribution to the freedom struggle was truly commendable and their ideas would live on long after the time, and would draw inspiration from the heroic deeds of the freedom fighters. By accepting death at the prime of their life, freedom fighters became a symbol of courage and sacrifice and secured a place in every Indian's heart for ever. We record our homage and deep admiration for the freedom fighters, which in the hour of peril for the motherland gave up the shelter of their homes and with unfailing courage and endurance stood shoulder to shoulder with their co-partners, in the frontline of India's national movement to share with them the sacrifices and triumphs of the struggle. The entire history of the freedom movement is replete with the saga of bravery, sacrifice and political sagacity of great men and women of the country.

Ram Prasad Bismil' (1897-1927) was one of the great Indian freedom fighter and well known as a great revolutionary poet in Hindi. In one poem he prays: "Even if I have to face death a thousand times for the sake of my motherland, I shall not be sorry. Oh Lord! Grant me a hundred births in Bharat. But grant me this, too, that each time I may give up my life in the service of the Mother land." In a poem written just before going to the gallows, he prays: "Oh Lord! Thy will be done. You are unique. Neither my tears nor I will endure. Grant me this boon, that to my last breath and the last drop of my blood, I may think of you and be immersed in your work." By and large, the general public have forgotten to remember the 'blood of the martyrs' and the poignant lyric of the patriot Ram Prasad Bismil: *Shahidon Ki Chitaon Par Lagenga Har Baras Mela, Vatan Par Marne Walon Ki Yehi Baki Nishan Hoga* (The annual fairs celebrating the patriot's martyrdom, shall be the symbols of their sacrifice), has not came true. Sixty four years after freedom, we find very few people devoted solely to the heroes and their deeds. The records of hero's of freedom movement since the 1857 struggle till independence picked and kept as an exhibit in the Cellular Jail as a symbolic of the scant regard we have paid to those martyrs who gave up their lives for India's freedom and there is no major nation in the world, which has paid so little attention to its saga of freedom struggle as India. In the last few years the Andaman administration and sons of freedom fighters made some efforts to recognize the sacrifices these brave Indians had made for the nation. There were men and women from all states and regions of India who fought for India's independence. Many were lauded; many went unnoticed. When they fought for independence, they did not fight for their region or people alone, but for the entire country. They had a dream of one big unified country where people could not only be free but truly united. And many of those freedom fighters gave up their lives because they believed in this dream.

REFERENCES

1. Amales Tripathi, Barun De, Bipan Chandra, *Freedom Struggle.*
2. Brown, Judith M., 'Gandhi and Civil Resistance in India, 1917-47', in Adam Roberts and Timothy Garton Ash (eds.), *Civil Resistance and Power Politics: The Experience of Non-violent Action from Gandhi to the Present.* Oxford & New York: Oxford University Press, 2009.
3. Chandler, Malcolm; Wright, John (2001). *Modern World History.* Heinemann Educational publishers. 2nd Review edition.
4. Collett, Nigel (2007 (New ed). *The Butcher of Amritsar: General Reginald Dyer.* Hambledon & London.
5. Gandhi, Mohandas (1993). *An Autobiography: The Story of My Experiments with Truth.* Boston: Beacon Press.
6. Majumdar, R.C. *History of the Freedom Movement in India.*
7. Philip Mason, *A Matter of Honour: An Account of the Indian Army, its Officers and Men.*
8. Sofri, Gianni (1995-1999). *Gandhi and India: A Century in Focus.* Janet Sethre Paxia (translator) (English edition translated from the Italian ed.). Gloucestershire: The Windrush Press.
9. Seal, Anil (1968). Emergence of Indian Nationalism: *Competition and Collaboration in the Later Nineteenth Century.* London: Cambridge U.P.

6
Conclusion

Andaman Islands is located in the middle of Bay of Bengal. It was significant in the struggle against the British Raj in the early twentieth century. The large number of Indian nationalists who participated in the armed struggle against the early British occupation and could not be accommodated in ordinary jails, were transferred here the British Government. A system of penal servitude with harsh punishment was established for them. The islands very closely connected with Indian Freedom Struggle for about a century. The history of the Andaman Islands began with the First War of Independence in 1857, the British Government thought of establishing a penal colony in Andaman. In March 1858, the first penal colony was established, with 200 prisoners, mostly rebels from the Indian Army. Initially the prisoners were kept in a jail at Viper island, which is about 15 minutes boat ride from Port Blair. The island had a jail, gallows, Kutcheri, Doctor's residence, etc. Subsequently, this Jail was abandoned and the Cellular Jail at Port Blair was constructed in 1906. During the time of successive Superintendents, E.H. Mann, General Steward, and Col. Cadell, the number of prisoners increased and they were subjected to inhuman tortures at the hands of the British jailors. Many changes, both in policy and practice, took place during Colonel Ferrar's time, which, inter alia, included concession to the convicts, mainland visit, etc.

Indeed the fundamental principles on which the penal system was founded in Andaman Islands was to bring reformative changes among the criminals particularly the hard core criminals and dacoits. The success of the colonial enterprise in the Andaman islands rested on transforming the transported convicts into a law-abiding and gainfully employed citizens of the British empire and converting the islands space into a flourishing agricultural colony. In the first half the conditions created the space for prison administration in Andaman seriously to explore the reform and rehabilitation of the criminals, even to the point of questioning whether the prison - the institution of long-term imprisonment could in fact reform. But in their attempt to restructure the system, the British regime chiefly failed because of its ill-deeds. The convict was firstly disciplined, secondly, it provided for wants of the settlement so far as they were supplied locally and thirdly, it was for the purpose of establishment of a colony and maintained for its strategic importance. Broadly speaking the penal settlement in Andamans was concerned with crime and its punishment in colonial India. There were serious problems with the manner in which the colonial state punished male and female offenders and few cases highlighted the quality of the system being implemented in remotest part of India. The penal authorities were under the impression that the voice of these prisoners would not travel beyond the islands. But to much of their annoyance, the convict prisoners successfully managed to dispatch secretly the news about sub-human living conditions, the tale of their sufferings and torture. The penal system in Andamans was repressive, is humiliated them. There was insubordination, homosexuality and general despondency among the convicts because of lack of personal and social ties and history rightly termed that Andamans as a 'hellish inferno', 'the land of death'. It also recounts the untold story of the Andamans penal order, where the prisoners experienced 'social death', the 'Kalapàani' known for brutality, violence and repression which have been associated with the history of the Andamans. In March 1868, 238 prisoners tried to escape. By April they were all caught. One committed suicide and of the remainder Superintendent Walker ordered 87 to be hanged.

The basic objective of the penal order in Andamans was

to teach the untaught, the stubborn and the defiant. To penetrate, indeed the penal authorities have used all such actions, which were termed inhuman and intolerable. Like any prison, the convicts were forced to do hard work and sometimes the authorities went beyond the purely punitive. The work that long-term convicts performed served certain ideological imperatives. In the context of criminality defined substantially, in terms of idleness of prison labour and vocational education aimed to train men and women in the moral value of work that was stable and visible, and that was properly subordinated to the authority of the British.

The freedom fighters that were brought to the Andaman Islands can be roughly divided into three phases. The first included the rebels of the 1857 struggle; the second the political prisoners between 1910 to 1921; and the third the political prisoners between 1932 to 1937. Records pertaining to the first phase are scanty or completely missing. However, it is known with certainty that Maulana Liquat Aly (Ali), the leader of 1857 struggle died here. The second phase of prisoners started with the Alipore conspiracy case in 1908. Except for Aurobindo Ghosh who was acquitted, the other four suspects were sentenced to transportation for life to these islands. In 1911, another well known name, Vinayak Damodar Savarkar of the Nasik Conspiracy case was sentenced to transportation for life. Noni Gopal Mukherjee was sentenced to 14 years of imprisonment and sent to the islands following the Dalhousie Square bomb case. The life these prisoners was extremely hard since they had to help run the daily affairs of the islands. They were expected to help in construction activities, keeping the settlement and the jail clean, and do many more activities in addition to these. But for all this, they still received very inhuman treatment from the British. This fact is amply illustrated by the suicide committed by Indu Bhushan Roy in 1912 (a young freedom fighter from Bengal). In another case, Ulaskar Dutt who was convicted in the Alipore Conspiracy, turned insane. Consequent to these tragic happenings, Ladha Ram who had edited the *Swarajya*, a nationalist weekly, went on hunger strike protesting against the prevailing inhuman conditions. In the following years, between 1913 and 1914, the jail saw further protests in the form of hunger strikes.

The prison was used by the British especially to exile political prisoners to the remote archipelago. Many notable freedom fighters such as Batukeshwar Dutt and Veer Savarkar, among others, were imprisoned here during the struggle for India's independence. Solitary confinement was implemented as the British government desired to ensure that political prisoners and revolutionaries be isolated from each other. The Andaman Island served as the ideal setting for the government to achieve this. Most prisoners of the Cellular Jail were independence activists. Some famous inmates of the Cellular Jail were Dr. Diwan Singh Kalepani, Maulana Fazl-e-Haq Khairabadi, Yogendra Shukla, Batukeshwar Dutt, Maulana Ahmadullah, Molvi Abdul Rahim Sadiqpuri, Babarao Savarkar, Vinayak Damodar Savarkar, Bhai Parmanand, V.O. Chidambaram Pillai, Subramaniam Shiva, Sohan Singh, Vaman Rao Joshi and Nand Gopal. Several revolutionaries tried in the Alipore Case (1908) such as Barindra Kumar Ghose, Upendra Nath Banerjee, Birendra Chandra Sen. Jatish Chandra Pal, the surviving companion of Bagha, Jatin, got demented under torture here. He was transferred to Berhampore Jail in Bengal, before his mysterious death in 1924.

Somewhere around this period the records tell us, Bhai Paramananda and Ashutosh Lahiri resorted to violent tactics and threw a European jailer down. By 1919-1920 things had deteriorated further and the Indian Jail Committee was appointed which finally decided to abolish the settlement and send all the prisoners back to the Indian mainland by 1921. Transportation resumed only in 1932 again and the number of prisoners hovered around 300. However, following the 1937 elections which were swept by the Indian National Congress, there was heavy unrest in the jails and mass protests by way of hunger strikes. Hunger strikes by the inmates during the early 1930s called attention to the inhuman conditions of their imprisonment. Mahatma Gandhi and Rabindranath Tagore intervened. The government decided to repatriate the political prisoners from the Cellular Jail in 1937-38.

The Cellular jail was mute witness to the sufferings and sacrifices of political prisoners for the cause of the motherland. Every Indian should feel proud of those sons who have given up the prime of their youth. Away from their homes and hearth, away from the love and affection of their near and dear ones, they had undergone tremendous hardships, atrocities and humiliation in far off, inhospitable climate. Their sole aim remained to free the motherland from foreign yoke. The Cellular jail gives the account of the intimidation and atrocities committed by the British regime in Andamans. The huge building instills terror in the minds of the onlookers and a sense of reverence. Every cell of the Jail tells a heart-rending story-the story of sufferings, sacrifices and indomitable spirit of resistance. The 'silence' system played havoc with the political freedom fighters. The high rate of insanity, delusions and suicide among the political prisoners attracted the political support and finally the British abandoned Cellular Jail system. By all accounts the Cellular Jail has become a holy place for all, particularly for younger generations to draw inspiration of sacrifice for the motherland.

World War II brought another series of changes in the life of the Andamans. During the War, the Japanese occupied Andamans on March 21, 1942 and kept the region under their effective control till October 8, 1945. Initially the Japanese behaved cordially towards the locals, but later became harsh and suspicious after instances came to their notice of some locals maintaining contacts with the British. As a result a large number of innocent people were killed. One such place where the massacre occurred was Humfreygunj. But one good result of the Japanese occupation was making the Andamans self-sufficient, at least in food production. The naval blockade created an acute food crisis and the Japanese compelled the local people to bring more land under cultivation. They also constructed roads. Netaji Subash Chandra Bose arrived in Port Blair on December 29, 1943 and was given a ceremonial welcome. He hoisted the National Flag at Port Blair on 30th Dec. 1943 for the first time during the British regime in India. During the war, Japanese soldiers had executed many Islanders, mainly educated and intelligent local borns on suspicion that they were British spies. A record reveals that, countless trials and mass executions took place, and hundreds of innocents were brought over from other islands on the pretext of rehabilitation, were pushed into the sea off Havelock Island. Many people are not aware of the Japanese brutalities particularly those of the Andaman and Nicobar Islands. It was a free for all. Men, women and children were shot dead or hacked by sword for no reason, the days of the wild Samurai, who had the power of life and death had returned to the Island. But historians and journalists have not made any effort to mark or highlight the mass killings of innocent people at Port Blair, complete devastation of an Andaman island, continuous suffering of the people for a period of three-and-a-half years as the. Meanwhile Japanese politicians and bureaucrats have made deliberate efforts to distort or cover up the facts of history. There was no end to atrocities till India won independence in 1947.

By all accounts the Andaman Islands have turned into a sacred place because of the sacrifices made by the freedom fighters. Immediately after independence, the 'Ex-Andaman Political Prisoners' Fraternity Circle' took up the issue with the Government of India for preserving the Cellular Jail as a National Memorial. The proposal was accepted, the jail was declared a National Memorial and on 11th February 1979, it was dedicated to the nation by the then Prime Minister, Morarji Desai, in the presence of a number of who had remained gaoled in this jail as political prisoners under the British regime. In his inaugural address, the prime minister had desired that a centre for research should also be started to understand and learn more about the lives of these patriots and on their contribution in the freedom struggle. The Ex-Andaman Political Prisoners' Fraternity Circle also desired that the record of case-history tickets of each freedom fighter imprisoned in the jail be prepared and kept in the jail library for future generations.

Indian accounts, however, paint a contrasting picture. From the time of its development in 1858, the settlement was first and foremost a repository for political prisoners. The Viper Chain Gang Jail on Viper Island was reserved for the worst of criminals and was also the site of prisoner hangings. In the twentieth century, it became a convenient place to house prominent members of India's independence movement, and it was here that on December 30, 1943, during Japanese occupation that the first flag of Indian independence was raised.

Guru Rabindra Nath once observed: Ò death is the true touchstone of genuine love. The only real test of such love is whether you are prepared to die for the sake of the object of your love Ó. It is beyond doubt that the political prisoners in the Andaman Islands successfully passed the supreme test. They were not only prepared, but also eager to die. Inhuman physical and mental tortures failed to deter them from their grim resolve to free their motherland. "Passionate love of Mother Bharati and National Leaders" and "hatred and disregard for the British Raj" and "emotional yearning for Freedom of India" pervaded the minds of political prisoners in Andaman. The Cellular jail became symbolic of the hardships faced by the Indians in their endeavour to attain freedom from their colonial rulers. The Cellular jail became infamous throughout the world for the inhuman treatment meted out to the inmates by the jail officials. This monument stands and reflects the tenacity of the Indians, who were struggling to attain freedom from the shackles of the British rule.

Annexure I

Details of Sentences Proclaimed and Sent to Andamans in Post-1857 Revolt

1. **RAMNAUTH,** Son of Rickhee Jee, Resident of Ammenabad, Lucknow: Marwaree Buneeach, Shopkeeper, 40 yrs, 5′.1", wheat colour, sentenced on 9th August′ 1858 for 7 years, transportation beyond the seas for possession of property obtained by rebellion. Sent to Andamans.
2. **SHEWDEEN,** Son of Buldee, Resident of Peera, Perg, Purtabgarh, U.P, Malee, servant, 35 yrs, 5′4", wheat colour, sentenced on 10th June 1858 for 5 years, transportation beyond the seas with iron and labour for acting as a spy. Sent to Andamans.
3. **MOHOMED BUX,** Son of Bhagoo, resident of village Purut, Lucknow: Sheikh, Mussulman Faker, 25ys, 5′ 4", dark complexion, sentenced on 10th June 1858 for 5 years transportation beyond the seas with irons and labour for acting as a spy. Sent to Andamans.
4. **KOONJ BEHAREE,** Son of Gunga Dass, Resident of village Dehat Lucnow, Jugdeshpoor: Brahmin, sepoy 63rd Regiment N.I., 36 years 5′8", wheat colour, sentenced on 13th April 1858 for 7years transportation beyond the seas with iron and labour for Mutiny. Sent to Andamans.
5. **ACKBUR ALLY,** Son of Mahaomed Roshim, Resident of Katawanee, Zillah Lucknow: Sheikh, Mossulman, cultivator, 75 , 5′8 ½″, dark complexion, sentenced on 4th May 1858 for 5 years transportation beyond the seas with irons and labour for Rebellion and breach of Arms Act. Sent to Andamans.

6. **KHODA BUX**, Son of Rumjun Ally, resident of village Kuthghuriah, Zillah Lucknow: Sheikh, Moosulman, cultivator, 25 years, 6'0", wheat colour, sentenced on 5th july 1858 for 5years transporation beyond the seas with irons and labour for rebellion. Sent to Andamans.

7. **KOOR SINGH**, Son of Dhoon Singh, resident of village Phogariah, Zillah Lucknow: Sheikh, Moosulman (religion ?) sepoy, Duffadar, 12th Irregular Cavalry, 45 years, 6'0", wheat colour, sentenced on 31st May 1858 for 7 years transportation beyond the seas with irons and labour for desertion. Sent to Andamans.

8. **MOHAMED JAN**, Son of Hidait Ally, resident of Peshwur: Moogul, no service, 36 years, 5'6-1/2", wheat colour, sentenced on 13th April 1858 for 14 years transportation beyond the seas with irons and labour for rebellion. Sent to Andamans.

9. **HURDEO SINGH,** Son of Davee Singh, resident of Nawabgunj, Zillah Cawnpore: Chutree, Hindoo, Sepoy sapper and miner, 35 years, 5'7" wheat colour, sentenced on 7th May 1858 for 14 years transportation beyond the seas with irons and labour for desertion. Sent to Andamans.

10. **GOWREE SHUNKER**, Son of Chhottoo, resident of villge Baikra, Perg, Hydergurh: Brahmin, pensioned artillery sepoy, 25 years, 5'6-1/2", dark complexion, sentenced on 19th April 1858 for transportation for life beyond the seas with irons and labour for rebellion. Sent to Andamans.

11. **JOWHIR SINGH**, Son of Than Singh, residnet of villge Kanah, Perg, Rascholee, Zillah, Poorwah: Chhutree, Hindoo, cultivator, 32 years, 5'7", wheat colour, sentenced on 16th July 1858 for 7 years transportation beyond the seas with irons and labour for rebellion and breach of Arms Act. Sent to Andamans.

12. **KEERUTH SINGH,** Son of Prem Singh, Residnet of village Kanah, Perg Rascholee, Zillah Poorwah: Chhutree, Hindoo, cultivator, 75 years, 6'2", wheat colour, sentenced on 18th July 1858 for 7 years transportation beyond the seas with irons and labour for rebellion and breach of Arms Act. Sent to Andamans.

13. **RUGHBUR SINGH,** Son of Zalim Singh, resident of Buxur: Chhutree, Hindoo, cultivator, 25 years , 5'10", wheat colour, sentenced on 22nd May 1858 for 14 years transportation beyond the seas for being accessory after the fact to the murder of Europeans. Sent to Andamans.

14. **MOOKTA SINGH,** Son of Drigapaul Singh, resident of village Kullunderpoor, Perg, Dowree Khera: Chhutree, Hindu, cultivator, 40 years , 5'5-1/2", wheat colour, sentenced on 22nd May 1858 for 14 years transportation beyond the seas with irons and labour for being accessory after the fact to the murder of Europeans. Sent to Andamans.

15. **JEET SINGH,** Son of Bechoo Singh, residnet of village Kullunderpoor, Perg, Dowree Khera: Chhutree, Hindoo, cultivator, 38 years , 5'6-1/2", wheat colour, sentenced on 22nd May 1858 for 14 years transportation beyond the seas with irons and labour for being accessory after the fact to the murder of Europeans. Sent to Andamans.

16. **PRAN NAUTH,** Son of Goolab Pandey, resident of Surrawa, Zillah Sooltanpoor: Brahmin, servant, 30 years, 5'7", wheat colour, sentenced on 23rd May 1858 for 14 years transportation beyond the seas with irons and labour for rebellion. Sent to Andamans.

17. **MUSHUR ALLY,** Son of Hoosein Bux, residnet of villge Kakoree, Zillah Lucknow: Sheikh, Moosulman, Tuhseeldar (Tehsildar), 58 years, 5'6", wheat colour, sentenced on 25th June 1858 for 7 years transportation beyond the seas with irons and labour for rebellion.

was formerly a Tehsildar in the Boolundsheher district. Sent to Andamans.

18. **JUGGUR NAUTH**, Son of Meebee Singh, resident of village Manhowra, Poorwah: Chhutree, Hindoo, Burkundauz, 50 years, 5'7-1/2", wheat colour, sentenced on 30th April 1858 for 7 years transportation with irons and labour for rebellion. No English or Persian warrant received – not mentioned with iron and labour. Sent to Andamans.

19. **KHOODA BUX**, Son of Badlu, resident of Poorwah Bijnour, Zillah Lucknow: Sheikh, Moosulman, Sepoy, Regiment not mentioned 33 years, 5'11-1/2", dark complexion, sentenced on 1st May 1858 for 7 years transportation for life with irons and labour for desertion and rebellion. Sent to Andamans.

20. **ENAYET ALLY,** *oorf* **MUNNEAH KHAN**, son of Juburuck Ally, resident of Sadeepoor Kullundurabad, Zillah Malslah (?). Puthan, Moosulman, Sepoy, Sapper and miner, 40 years, 5'9", wheat colour, sentenced on 5th May 1858 for transportation for life with irons and labour for mutiny. Sent to Andamans.

21. **MUKBOOL SHAH**, Son of Ghazee Khanm resident of Lucknow: Fakeer, Moosulman, 30 years, 5'5-1/2", dark complexion, sentenced on 18th June 1858 for transportation for life with irons and labour for abduction and rape of a Christiain girl. Sent to Andamans.

22. **BHOWANY DEEN**, Son of Hoolasee, resident of Shahdutgunj, Lucknow: Kulwar, Shephered, 30 years, 5'5-1/2", wheat colour, sentenced on 24th June 1858 for 7 years transportation beyond the seas with irons and labour for rebellion and breach of Arms Act. Sent to Andamans.

23. **RAMDEEN**, Son of Khuggesur, resident of village Burrownee thana Goshaeengunj, Lucknow: Pasee,

Labour, 25 years, 5'5", wheat colour, sentenced on 12th July 1858 for 7 years transportation beyond the seas with irons and labour for rebellion and willful murder and wandering with interest to murder. Sent to Andamans.

24. **PUNCHUM SINGH**, Son of Gya Deen, residnet of village Guddree Kheriah: Chhutree, Hindoo, Sepoy of Nadreeka Pultun, Oudh force 45 years , 6'1-1/2", wheat colour, sentenced on 17th May 1858 for transportation for life beyond the seas with irons and labour for mutiny and rebellion. Sent to Andamans.

Details of Political Prisoners sent to Andamans in Post-1900 Revolt

25. **Bhan Singh** : A convict of Lahore Conspiracy case who was most brutally assaulted for alleged misbehaviour with the Superintendent of Andaman Cellular Jail. He died during hunger strike.

26. **Ram Rakha** : Died during hunger strike in 1919 in Andaman Cellular Jail.

27. **Dinesh Gupta,** S/o Satish : Died during hunger strike in 1919 in Andaman Cellular Jail.

28. **Mahabir Singh,** S/o Kunwar Devi Singh : Etah District. (U.P.). Born Sept. 16, 1904 and died on May 17, 1933 in Andaman Cellular Jail in course of a hunger strike while resisting forced-feeding.

29. **Man Krishna Namadas (Mohan Kishore)**, Mymensingh (now in Bangladesh) : resorted to hunger strike in Andaman Cellular Jail as a protest against inhuman treatment on political prisoners died on May 26, 1933 while resisting forced-feeding.

30. **Mohit Maitra,** S/o Hem Chandra Maitra : Calcutta, West Bengal. Died on May 28, 1933 in Andaman Cellular Jail in course of hunger strike while resisting forced-feeding.

31. **Haren Munshi :** Died on Jan. 30, 1938 in Dacca Jail (now in Bangladesh) while resisting force-feeding in course of a hunger strike resorted to by repatriated Andaman prisoners convicted in Titagar Conspiracy case.

Annexure II

Freedom Fighters Deported to Andamans in Connection with First War of Independence, 1857

Sl. No.	*Name of the Political Prisoners*	*Native place/ State*
1.	Alama Fazal Huque	U.P.
2.	Bahadur Goonburah	Assam
3.	Bahadur Singh	M.P.
4.	Bhim Nayek	M.P.
5.	Devi	M.P.
6.	Dutiram Barua	Assam
7.	Dudhnath Tiwari	U.P
8.	Futta	M.P.
9.	Garabdas Patel	Gujrat
10.	Gulab Khan	M.P.
11.	Hatte Singh	Orissa
12.	Himanohal Singh	U.P.
13.	Jawahar Singh	M.P.
14.	Kura Singh	U.P.
15.	Liaqat Ali	U.P.
16.	Loney Singh	U.P.
17.	Madhu Mallik	Assam
18.	Maulvi Syed Aluddin	Hyderabad
19.	Mahibullah	M.P.
20.	Manju Shah	M.P.

21.	Maya Ram	M.P.
22.	Mir Jafar Ali	Thanseswari
23.	Narayan	Bihar
24.	Noora	M.P.
25.	Niranjan Singh	
26.	Qaim Khan	M.P.
27.	Sirajuddin	M.P.
28.	Seikh Formud Ali	Assam
29.	Venkat Roa	M.P.

Wahabi Rebels Deported to Andamans (1860 - 1870)

30.	Ahmadulla	Patan Trial, 1865
31.	Amiruddin	Maldah Trial, 1870
32.	Ibrahim Mandal	Rajmahal Trial, 1870
33.	Md. Sher Ali	
34.	Yahya Ali	Ambala Trial, 1864

Moplah Rebels Deported to Andamans (1922 - 1924)

35.	Neliiparamban Alavi Haji	Kerala
36.	Kolaparamban Kunjalavi	Kerala
37.	Kozhisseri Koya Kutty	Kerala
38.	Ambattuparamban Saidalippa	Kerala
39.	Kayakkatiparambil Kunjeni	Kerala
40.	Machingal Rayin	Kerala
41.	Kuthukallan Kunjara	Kerala
42.	Chungath Athan	Kerala
43.	Variyath Valappil Ahammed Kutty	Kerala
44.	Mattummal Ahammed Kutty	Kerala
45.	Pooyikunnan Marakkar	Kerala
46.	Machincheri Alavi	Kerala

47.	Pokat Koyami	Kerala
48.	Puthampeedikayil Kunjikader Molla	Kerala
49.	Mukri Kunjayammu	Kerala
50.	Poolakuyyil Kunhi Moideen Kutty	Kerala
51.	Poovakundil Alavi	Kerala
52.	Neehiyil Kunjeedu	Kerala
53.	Aripra Pocker	Kerala
54.	Mattummal Marakkar	Kerala
55.	Chakkupurakkal Kutty Hasan	Kerala

Freedom Fighters Incarcerated in Cellular Jail 1909-1921

56.	Daji Narayan Joshi	Bombay
57.	Ganesh Damodar Savarkar	Bombay
58.	Vinayak Damodar Savarkar	Bombay
59.	Ali Ahmed Siddiqui	Punjab
60.	Amar Singh	Punjab
61.	Bhai Paramanand	Punjab
62.	Bhan Singh	Punjab
63.	Bishen Singh	Punjab
64.	Bishen Singh	Punjab
65.	Bishen Singh	Punjab
66.	Bishen Singh	Punjab
67.	Channan Singh	Punjab
68.	Chattar Singh	Punjab
69.	Chattar Singh	Punjab
70.	Chet Ram	Punjab
71.	Chuher Singh	Punjab
72.	Gurudah Singh	Punjab

73.	Gurudit Singh	Punjab
74.	Gurumukh Singh	Punjab
75.	Gurumukh Singh	Punjab
76.	Hardit Singh	Punjab
77.	Harnam Singh	Punjab
78.	Hazara Singh	Punjab
79.	Hidaram	Punjab
80.	Hirda Singh	Punjab
81.	Inder Singh	Punjab
82.	Inder Singh	Punjab
83.	Jagat Ram	Punjab
84.	Jawand Singh	Punjab
85.	Jawla Singh	Punjab
86.	Jiwan Singh	Punjab
87.	Kala Singh	Punjab
88.	Kala Singh	Punjab
89.	Kapur Singh	Punjab
90.	Kartar Singh	Punjab
91.	Kehr Singh	Punjab
92.	Kehr Singh	Punjab
93.	Kesar Singh	Punjab
94.	Kirpa Singh	Punjab
95.	Kirpal Singh	Punjab
96.	Kusal Singh	Punjab
97.	Lakhan Singh	Punjab
98.	Lal Singh	Punjab
99.	Lal Singh	Punjab
100.	Madan Singh	Punjab
101.	Mangal Singh	Punjab

102.	Manohar Singh	Punjab
103.	Munsha Singh	Punjab
104.	Nand Singh	Punjab
105.	Nand Singh	Punjab
106.	Natha Singh	Punjab
107.	Nehar Singh	Punjab
108.	Nidhan Singh	Punjab
109.	Piara Singh	Punjab
110.	Prithwi Singh Azad	Punjab
111.	Raja Ram	Punjab
112.	Ram Raksha Bhale	Punjab
113.	Ram Saran Das	Punjab
114.	Randhir Singh	Punjab
115.	Roda Singh	Punjab
116.	Rulla Singh	Punjab
117.	Rurh Singh	Punjab
118.	Sajjan Singh	Punjab
119.	Saon Singh	Punjab
120.	Sher Singh	Punjab
121.	Shingara Singh	Punjab
122.	Shiv Singh	Punjab
123.	Sohan Singh	Punjab
124.	Sucha Singh	Punjab
125.	Surain Singh	Punjab
126.	Surjan Singh	Punjab
127.	Teja Singh	Punjab
128.	Thakkar Singh	Punjab
129.	Udhem Singh	Punjab
130.	Wasakha Singh	Punjab

131.	Waswa Singh	Punjab
132.	Govinda Ram	United Province
133.	Hoti Lal	United Province
134.	Ladha Ram	United Province
135.	Mukhada Babu	United Province
136.	Mujtaba Husain	United Province
137.	Nandgopal	United Province
138.	Paramanand (Jhanshi)	United Province
139.	Ram Hari	United Province
140.	Roshan Lal	United Province
141.	Sachindra Nath Sanyal	United Province
142.	Abani Bhuan Chakrabarti	Bengal
143.	Abinash Bhattacharji	Bengal
144.	Amrita Lal Hazra	Bengal
145.	Ashutosh Lahiri	Bengal
146.	Aswani Kumar Basu	Bengal
147.	Barindra Kumar Ghosh	Bengal
148.	Bhupendra Nath Ghosh	Bengal
149.	Bibhuti Bhusan Sarkar	Bengal
150.	Bidhu Bhusan Dey	Bengal
151.	Bidhu Bhusan Sarkar	Bengal
152.	Siren Sen	Bengal
153.	Brojendra Nath Datta	Bengal
154.	Gobinda Chandra Kar	Bengal
155.	Gopendra Lal Roy	Bengal
156.	Harendra Bhattacharjee	Bengal
157.	Hem Chandra Das (Kanungo)	Bengal
158.	Hrishikesh Kanjilal	Bengal
159.	Indu Bhusan Roy	Bengal

160.	Jatindra Nath Nandi	Bengal
161.	Jyotish Chandra Paul	Bengal
162.	Kalidas Ghosh	Bengal
163.	Khagendra Nath Chaudhuri	Bengal
164.	Kinuram Pal	Bengal
165.	Kshitish Chandra Sanyal	Bengal
166.	Madan Mohan Bhowmik	Bengal
167.	Nagendra Nath Chanda	Bengal
168.	Nagendra Nath Sarkar	Bengal
169.	Nani Gopal Mukherji	Bengal
170.	Naren Ghosh Chaudhuri	Bengal
171.	Nikhil Ranjan Guha Roy	Bengal
172.	Nikunja Behari Pal	Bengal
173.	Nirapada Roy	Bengal
174.	Phani Bhusan Roy	Bengal
175.	Pulin Behari Das	Bengal
176.	Sachindra Nath Datta	Bengal
177.	Sachindra Lal Mitra	Bengal
178.	Sanukul Chatterji	Bengal
179.	Satish Chandra Chatterji Bhattacharji	Bengal
180.	Satya Ranjan Basu	Bengal
181.	Sudhir Chandra Dey	Bengal
182.	Sudhir Kumar Sarkar	Bengal
183.	Surendra Nath Biswas	Bengal
184.	Suresh Chandra Sengupta	Bengal
185.	Trailakya Chakrabarti	Bengal
186.	Ullash Kar Datta	Bengal
187.	Upendra Nath Banerji	Bengal

Freedom Fighters Incarcerated in Cellular Jail (1922-1932)

188.	Lakshmi Kanta Shukla	United Province
189.	Vishnu Saran Dublis	United Province
190.	Kotaya Korrabu	Madras
191.	Pandu Padal Bonangi	Madras
192.	Sanyasayya Golivilli	Madras
193.	Sanyasi Kunchatti	Madras
194.	Satyanarayan Raju	Madras
195.	Virayya Dora Taggi	Madras
196.	Satyanarayan Raju	Madras

Freedom Fighters Incarcerated in Cellular Jail 1932-1938

197.	Hazari Singh	Punjab
198.	Kushiram Mehta	Punjab
199.	Dhwantari	Delhi
200.	Harabandhu Samajdar	Delhi
201.	Bachu Lal	United Province
202.	Batukeshwar Datta	United Province
203.	Bijoy Kumar Sinha	United Province
204.	Gaya Prasad	United Province
205.	Jaidev Kapoor	United Province
206.	Kundan Lal Gupta	United Province
207.	Mahavir Singh	United Province
208.	Prem Prakash	United Province
209.	Ram Singh Dogra	United Province
210.	Shambhu Nath Azad	United Province
211.	Sheo Verma	United Province
212.	Biswanath Mathur	Bihar
213.	Chandrika Singh	Bihar
214.	Gouri Shankar Dubey	Bihar

215.	Gulab Chand Gupta	Bihar
216.	Jogendra Shukul	Bihar
217.	Kamal Nath Tiwari	Bihar
218.	Kanhaiya Lal Misir	Bihar
219.	Kedarmoni Shukul	Bihar
220.	Kesho Prasad	Bihar
221.	Mihabir Misir	Bihar
222.	Malay Bramachari	Bihar
223.	Mohit Adhikari	Bihar
224.	Nanku Singh	Bihar
225.	Pramatha Nath Ghosh	Bihar
226.	Ram Pratap Singh	Bihar
227.	Shyam Krishna Agarwal	Bihar
228.	Shyama Charan Bharatwar	Bihar
229.	Shyamdeo Narayan alias Ram Singh	Bihar
230.	Suraj Nath Chaure	Bihar

Annexure III

Bengali Freedom Fighters Incarcerated in Cellular Jail 1932-1938

S.l.No	*Name of the Political Prisoners*	*Native place/ State*
1.	Abani Ranjan Ghosh	Bengal
2.	Abani Mukherji	Bengal
3.	Abdul Kader Chaudhuri	Bengal
4.	Abhaypada Mukherji	Bengal
5.	Achyute Ghatak	Bengal
6.	Adhir Ranjan Nag	Bengal
7.	Adhir Chandra Sinha	Bengal
8.	Ajay Sinha	Bengal
9.	Ajit Kumar Mitra	Bengal
10.	Akshay Kuamr Mitra	Bengal
11.	Amalendu Bagchi	Bengal
12.	Amar Mukherji	Bengal
13.	Amar Suthradhar	Bengal
14.	Amritendu Mukherji	Bengal
15.	Amulya Kumar Mitra	Bengal
16.	Amulya Roy	Bengal
17.	Amulya Chandra Sen Gupta	Bengal
18.	Ananda Prasad Gupta	Bengal
19.	Ananta Bhattacharji	Bengal
20.	Ananta Chakrabarti Bhola	Bengal

21.	Ananta Kumar Chakarabarti	Bengal
22.	Anata Dey	Bengal
23.	Ananta Kukherji	Bengal
24.	Ananta Lal Singh	Bengal
25.	Anath Bandhu Saha	Bengal
26.	Anil Mukherji	Bengal
27.	Annada Charan Pal	Bengal
28.	Anukul Chatrerji	Bengal
29.	Arabinda Dey	Bengal
30.	Atul Chandra Datta	Bengal
31.	Bangeswar Roy	Bengal
32.	Bankim Chakrabarti	Bengal
33.	Barindra Kumar Ghosh	Bengal
34.	Benoy Kumar Basu	Bengal
35.	Benoy Bhusan Roy	Bengal
36.	Benoy Tarafdar	Bengal
37.	Bhanba Ranjan Patutunqu	Bengal
38.	Bhabatosh Kurmakar	Bengal
39.	Bhabesh Talukdar	Bengal
40.	Bhagwan Chandra Biswas	Bengal
41.	Bharat Sharma Roy	Bengal
42.	Bholanath Roy	Bengal
43.	Bhubon Mohon Chandra	Bengal
44.	Bhupal Chandra Basu	Bengal
45.	Bhupal Chandra Panda	Bengal
46.	Bhupendra Chandra Bhattachraji	Bengal
47.	Bhupesh Chandra Nanergi	Bengal
48.	Bhupesh Chandra Guha	Bengal
49.	Bhupesh Chandra Saha	Bengal

50.	Bibhuti Bhusan Banerji	Bengal
51.	Bidhu Bhusan Guha Biswas	Bengal
52.	Bidhu Bhusan Sen	Bengal
53.	Bidyadhar Saha	Bengal
54.	Bijan Kumar Saha	Bengal
55.	Bijay Kumar Sen	Bengal
56.	Bijay Krishna Bunerji	Bengal
57.	Bimal Chandra Bhattacharji	Bengal
58.	Bimal Bhowmik	Bengal
59.	Bimal Dasgupta	Bengal
60.	Bimal Kumar Sarkar	Bengal
61.	Bimalendu Chakrabarti	Bengal
62.	Biraj Deb	Bengal
63.	Biren Chaudhuri	Bengal
64.	Birendra Chandra Lahiri	Bengal
65.	Biren Roy	Bengal
66.	Biru Bhusan Chakrabarti	Bengal
67.	Chandra Kanta Bhattacharji	Bengal
68.	Chitta Biswas	Bengal
69.	Chittaranjon Datta	Bengal
70.	Chintaharan Das	Bengal
71.	Chunilal Deb	Bengal
72.	Deb Kumar Das	Bengal
73.	Debendra Talukdar	Bengal
74.	Bharani Banik	Bengal
75.	Dharani Biswas	Bengal
76.	Dharani Chakrabarti	Bengal
77.	Dharanidhar Roy	Bengal
78.	Dhirendra Kumar Biswas	Bengal

79.	Bhiren Chaudhuri	Bengal
80.	Dhiren Datta	Bengal
81.	Dhirendra Nath Bhattacharji	Bengal
82.	Dhirendra Chakrabarti Comilla	Bengal
83.	Dhirendra Chandra Chakrabarti Mymensingh	Bengal
84.	Dhirendra Chandra Das	Bengal
85.	Dhrubesh Chatterji	Bengal
86.	Dinesh Banik	Bengal
87.	Dinesh Chandra Das Mymensigh	Bengal
88.	Dinesh Chand'a Das	Bengal
89.	Dinesh Dasgupta	Bengal
90.	Dinesh Dhar	Bengal
91.	Dinesh Chandra Saha	Bengal
92.	Durga Sankar Das	Bengal
93.	Dwijendra Nath Naha	Bengal
94.	Dwijendra Nath Talapatra	Bengal
95.	Fakir Chandra Sen Gupta	Bengal
96.	Gagan Chandra Dey	Bengal
97.	Ganesh Chandra Ghosh	Bengal
98.	Gobinda Kar	Bengal
99.	Gobinda Prasad Bera	Bengal
100.	Gomiruddin Sarkar	Bengal
101.	Gopal Acharji	Bengal
102.	Gopal Chandra Deb	Bengal
103.	Gopi Mohan Saha	Bengal
104.	Gour Gopal Datta	Bengal
105.	Haran Chandra Deb	Bengal
106.	Harekrisna Konar	Bengal

107.	Harendra Nath Das Mandal	Bengal
108.	Haribal Chakrabarti	Bengal
109.	Haridas Saha	Bengal
110.	Harihar Datta	Bengal
111.	Haripada Banerji	Bengal
112.	Haripada Basu	Bengal
113.	Haripada Bhattacharji	Bengal
114.	Haripada Chaudhuri	Bengal
115.	Haripada Dey	Bengal
116.	Hem Chandra Bakshi	Bengal
117.	Hemendra Nath Chakrabarti	Bengal
118.	Hem Chandra Datta	Bengal
119.	Himangshu Bhowmik	Bengal
120.	Hiramohan Chatterji	Bengal
121.	Hriday Das Faridpur	Bengal
122.	Hriday Das chittagang	Bengal
123.	Hrishikesh Basu	Bengal
124.	Hrishikesh Bhattacharji	Bengal
125.	Hrishikesh Datta	Bengal
126.	Indu Bhusan Das	Bengal
127.	Jagadananda Mukherji	Bengal
128.	Jagat Basu	Bengal
129.	Jagat Roy	Bengal
130.	Jamini Kumar Dey	Bengal
131.	Jangeswar Das	Bengal
132.	Janaki Nath Das	Bengal
133.	Jatindra Dey	Bengal
134.	Jayesh Chandra Bhattacharji	Bengal
135.	Jiban Guha Thakurta	Bengal

136.	Jiban Molla	Bengal
137.	Jibendra Kumar Das	Bengal
138.	Jitendra Nath Chakrabarti	Bengal
139.	Jitendra Nath Gupta	Bengal
140.	Jitendra Majumdar	Bengal
141.	Jnanda Gobinda Gupta	Bengal
142.	Jogendra Chakrabarti	Bengal
143.	Jogendra Mohan Guha	Bengal
144.	Jogesh Chakrabarti	Bengal
145.	Jogesh Chandra Das	Bengal
146.	Jyotirmay Roy	Bengal
147.	Jyotish Majumdar	Bengal
148.	Kalachand Chakrabarti	Bengal
149.	Kali Mohan Bajerji	Bengal
150.	Kalipada Bhattacharji	Bengal
151.	Kali Kinkar Dey	Bengal
152.	Kalipada Chakrobarti	Bengal
153.	Kalipada Roy	Bengal
154.	Kaliprasanna Roy Choudhuri	Bengal
155.	Kamakshya Charan Ghosh	Bengal
156.	Shri Kamal Srimani	Bengal
157.	Kamini Dey	Bengal
158.	Kartik Charan Ghosh Paresh	Bengal
159.	Kartik Sarkar	Bengal
160.	Kaumudi Kanta Bhattacharji	Bengal
161.	Keshab Lal Chatterji	Bengal
162.	Keshab Samajdar	Bengal
163.	Kiran Dey	Bengal
164.	Kiriti Bhusan Majumdar	Bengal

165.	Khoka Roy Sudhindra Kumar	Bengal
166.	Kripanath Dey	Bengal
167.	Krishna Biswas	Bengal
168.	Krishnapada Chakrabarti	Bengal
169.	Kshitish Chandra Chaudhuri	Bengal
170.	Kshitish Chandra Roy	Bengal
171.	Kumud Mukherji	Bengal
172.	Kumudini Ghosh	Bengal
173.	Loke Nath Bal	Bengal
174.	Lalt Chakrabarti	Bengal
175.	Lalit Chandra Raha	Bengal
176.	Lalit Singh	Bengal
177.	Lal Mohan Sen	Bengal
178.	Modan Roy Chaudhuri	Bengal
179.	Madhu Banerji	Bengal
180.	Madhusudan Datta	Bengal
181.	Md. Ibrahim Alias Tarapada	Bengal
182.	Mahendra Bhawmik	Bengal
183.	Mahesh Barua	Bengal
184.	Makhan Dey	Bengal
185.	Mani Lal Datta	Bengal
186.	Mani Ramani Ganguli	Bengal
187.	Manindra Lal Chaudhuri	Bengal
188.	Manindra Dey	Bengal
189.	Manindra Chandra Sen	Bengal
190.	Manmatha Datta	Bengal
191.	Man Mohan Saha	Bengal
192.	Manoranjan Banerji	Bengal
193.	Monoranjan Chaudhuri	Bengal

194.	Manoranjan Guha Thakurta	Bengal
195.	Mathura Nath Datta	Bengal
196.	Mohan Lal Nag	Bengal
197.	Mohan Kishore Namadas	Bengal
198.	Mohit Mohan Namadas	Bengal
199.	Mokshada Ranjan Chakrabarty	Bengal
200.	Mritunjay Banerji	Bengal
201.	Mukul Ranjan Sen	Bengal
202.	Murari Goswami	Bengal
203.	Magen Dasgupta	Bengal
204.	Nagendra Deb	Bengal
205.	Nagendra Nath Dey	Bengal
206.	Nagendra Nath Gupta	Bengal
207.	Nagen Modak	Bengal
208.	Nagendra Mohan Mustafi	Bengal
209.	Nalini Sengupta	Bengal
210.	Nanda Lal Das Gupta	Bengal
211.	Nanda Dulal Singh	Bengal
212.	Nani Gopal Das	Bengal
213.	Nani Das Gupta	Bengal
214.	Narayan Chandra Roy	Bengal
215.	Nalini Das	Bengal
216.	Narendra Nath Das	Bengal
217.	Narendra Chandra Ghosh	Bengal
218.	Narendra Prasad Ghosh	Bengal
219.	Nepal Sarkar	Bengal
220.	Nibaran Chakrabarti	Bengal
221.	Niranjan Sen	Bengal
222.	Nirendra Barua	Bengal
223.	Nirmalendu Guha	Bengal
224.	Nishakanta Roy Chaudhuri	Bengal

225.	Nitya Ranjan Chaudhuri	Bengal
226.	Nripendra Datta Roy	Bengal
227.	Paresh Chandra Chaudhuri	Bengal
228.	Paresh Chandra Guha	Bengal
229.	Parimal Chandra Ghosh	Bengal
230.	Phani Bhusan Das Gupta	Bengal
231.	Phani Nandy	Bengal
232.	Prabir Kumar Goswami	Bengal
233.	Prafulla Kumar Biswas	Bengal
234.	Prafulla Bhawmik	Bengal
235.	Prafulla Kumar Majumdar	Bengal
236.	Prafulla Narayan Sanyal	Bengal
237.	Prakash Chandra Sett	Bengal
238.	Pran Gopal Mukherji	Bengal
239.	Pran Krishna Chakrabarti	Bengal
240.	Pran Krishna Chaudhuri	Bengal
241.	Prasanta Kumar Sengupta	Bengal
242.	Pravash Kumar Roy	Bengal
243.	Priyada Ranjan Chakrabarti	Bengal
244.	Probodh Kumar Roy	Bengal
245.	Prodyot Roy Chudhuri	Bengal
246.	Promode Ranjan Basu	Bengal
247.	Provakar Biruni	Bengal
248.	Provat Chandra Chakrabarti	Bengal
249.	Provat Kumar Ghosh	Bengal
250.	Provat Mitra	Bengal
251.	Purna Goswami	Bengal
252.	Purnendu Sekhar Guha	Bengal
253.	Robindra Banerji	Bengal
254.	Rabindra Banerji	Bengal
255.	Rabindra Chandra Neogi	Bengal

256.	Radha Ballav Gope	Bengal
257.	Radhika Dey Das	Bengal
258.	Rajani Kant Sarkar	Bengal
259.	Rajat Bhusan Datta	Bengal
260.	Rajendra Nath Charkrabarti	Bengal
261.	Raj Mohan Karanjai	Bengal
262.	Rakhal Chandra Dev	Bengal
263.	Rakhal Das Mallik	Bengal
264.	Ram Chandra Das	Bengal
265.	Ramendra Nath Samajdar	Bengal
266.	Ramesh Chatterji	Bengal
267.	Ramesh Chandra Roy	Bengal
268.	Ramkrishna Sarkar	Bengal
269.	Ranadhir Das Gupta	Bengal
270.	Reboti Mohan Saha	Bengal
271.	Sachindra Chandra Home	Bengal
272.	Sachindra Lal Kar Gupta	Bengal
273.	Sachindra Nath Mitra	Bengal
274.	Sachindra Nandi	Bengal
275.	Sailesh Datta	Bengal
276.	Sailesh Chandra Roy	Bengal
277.	Samadish Chandra Roy	Bengal
278.	Samarendra Ghosh	Bengal
279.	Sanatan Roy	Bengal
280.	Santipada Chakrabatti	Bengal
281.	Santi Gopal Sen	Bengal
282.	Santosh Kumar Datta	Bengal
283.	Sarada Prasanna Basu	Bengal
284.	Saradindu Bhattacharji	Bengal
285.	Sarat Dhupi Das	Bengal
286.	Saroj Kumar Basu	Bengal

287.	Saroj Guha	Bengal
288.	Daroj Roy	Bengal
289.	Sarasi Mohan Moitra	Bengal
290.	Sashi Mohan Bhattacharji	Bengal
291.	Satish Chandra Sasu	Bengal
292.	Satish Chandra Pakrashi	Bengal
293.	Satyabrata Chakrabarti	Bengal
294.	Satya Ranjan Ghosh	Bengal
295.	Satyendra Kumar Basu	Bengal
296.	Satyendra Narayan Majumdar	Bengal
297.	Sarajul Huque	Bengal
298.	Shahaya Ram Das	Bengal
299.	Sachin Chakarabarti	Bengal
300.	Sitangsu Datta Roy	Bengal
301.	Sridhar Goswami	Bengal
302.	Subal Chandra Roy	Bengal
303.	Subodh Chaudhuri	Bengal
304.	Subodh Roy	Bengal
305.	Sudhangsu Dasgupta Babu	Bengal
306.	Sadhangsu Sasgupta Manu	Bengal
307.	Sudhangsu Sasgupta (Bankura)	Bengal
308.	Sudhangsu Lahiri	Bengal
309.	Sudhangsu Sengupta	Bengal
310.	Sudhendu Chandra Dam	Bengal
311.	Sudhindra Nath Bhattacharji	Bengal
312.	Sudhindra Roy	Bengal
313.	Sudhir Bhattachrji	Bengal
314.	Sudhir Chaudhuri	Bengal
315.	Sudhir Kumar Roy	Bengal
316.	Sudhir Kumar Samajdar	Bengal
317.	Sukhendu Bikash Dastidar	Bengal

318.	Sukumar Ghosh	Bengal
319.	Sukumar Sengupta	Bengal
320.	Sunil Kumar Chatterji	Bengal
321.	Sunirmal Sen	Bengal
322.	Suren Acharji	Bengal
323.	Suren Banik	Bengal
324.	Surendra Nath Datta	Bengal
325.	Surendra Nath Datta Gupta	Bengal
326.	Surendra Dhar Chaudhuri	Bengal
327.	Surendra Mohan Kar Roy	Bengal
328.	Suren Surkhel	Bengal
329.	Suresh Chandra Das	Bengal
330.	Sushil Kumar Banerji	Bengal
331.	Sushil Kumar Chakrabarti	Bengal
332.	Sushil Dasgupta	Bengal
333.	Sushil Kumar Dey	Bengal
334.	Uma Sankar Konar	Bengal
335.	Umesh Khudiram Bhattacharji	Bengal
336.	Upendra Nath Mandal	Bengal
337.	Upen Saha	Bengal
338.	Usha Ranjan Dey	Bengal
339.	Benoy Laskar	Assam
340.	Gopen Roy	Assam
341.	Gouranga Mohan Das	Assam
342.	Motilal Roy	Assam
343.	Satyendra Roy	Assam
344.	Prativadi Bhayankara Venkatchary	Andhra
345.	T. Satchidananda Sivam	Andhra

Annexure IV

Rulers of Andaman Islands till 1947

S.No.	*Name of the Officer*	*Tenure*
1.	Dr. James Pettison Walker	1858-1859
2.	Captain Haughton	1859-1862
3.	R.L. Tytler	1862-1864
4.	Lt. Col. Ford	1864-1868
5.	Col H. Man	1868-1871
6.	Major D.M. Stewart	1871-1872
7.	General Shri Donald Martin Stewart, CGB, GCSI, CIE	1872-1875
8.	Major General C.A. Barwell IA	1875-1879
9.	Col. T. Cadel, VCIA	1879-1892
10.	Col N.H. Horsford, IA	1892-1894
11.	Col Sir Richard C Temple, IA	1894-1903
12.	Mr. F.E. Tuson	1903-1904
13.	Mr. W.R.H. Merk, CSI	1904-1906
14.	Lt. Col. H.A. Browing, IA	1906-1913
15.	Lt. Col. MW Doughlas, IA	1913-1920
16.	Col. H.C. Beaddon IA	1920-1923
17.	Lt. Col ML Ferrar KCSI, CSI, CIE, IA	1923-1931
18.	Mr. J.W. Smyth, ICS	1931-1935
19.	W.A. Consgrave, CIE, ICS	1935-1938
20.	Sir C.E. Waterfall CIE, IP, ICS (he was taken as prisoner by Japanese)	1938-1942
21.	**JAPANESE OCCUPATION** :	23-3-1942 to 06-10-1945
22.	Mr N.K. Paterson OBE, ICS	1945-1947

Index

C